8.95

D0969684

POLITICS IN THE SOVIET UNION

FROM BREZHNEV TO GORBACHEV

Other Ti...

Politics in...
Politics in...
Politics in France • From Charles de...
Politics in the United States...
Politics in West Germany...

About the Series

Chambers Political Spotlights ... between a
conventional textbook and ... Each title
examines the key political ... of the
country, providing ... background to
each development...

DISCARD

Other titles in this Series

About the Series

Chambers Political Spotlights aim to provide a bridge between conventional textbooks and contemporary reporting. Each title examines the key political, economic and social changes of the country, providing, in addition, a brief contextual background to each development discussed.

CHAMBERS POLITICAL SPOTLIGHTS

THE

POLITICS IN

SOVIET UNION

FROM BREZHNEV TO GORBACHEV

Ian Derbyshire
Ph.D. Cantab

Chambers

First published by Sandpiper Publishing as a Sandpiper Compact, 1985
This edition published by W & R Chambers Ltd, 1987
Reprinted 1988

British Library Cataloguing in Publication Data

Derbyshire, Ian
  Politics in the Soviet Union: from
  Brezhnev to Gorbachev.—(Chambers
  political spotlights).
  1. Soviet Union—Politics and
  government—1953-
  I.Title
  320.947   JN6531

  ISBN 0-550-20745-7

Typeset by Bookworm Typesetting Limited, 9a Gayfield Square, Edinburgh
Printed in Great Britain at the University Press, Cambridge

Acknowledgements

This book is based on a wide range of contemporary sources including
*The Times, The Guardian, The Independent, The Observer, The Sunday
Times, The Economist, Newsweek, Time, Keesing's Contemporary
Archives, The Annual Register* and *Europa: A World Survey.*

Figure 3 by permission of *The Economist*

Every effort has been made to trace copyright holders, but if any have
inadvertently been overlooked the publishers will be pleased to make the
necessary arrangements at the first opportunity.

Contents

Preface

The years since 1980 have seen the greatest changes in the Soviet Union since the early 1960s. The long Brezhnev era finally came to an end in November 1982, leaving the Soviet Union established as a superpower but faced with problems of economic stagnation at home and mounting popular unrest on its borders. Two shortlived administrations followed in the space of less than three years – those led by Yuri Andropov and Konstantin Chernenko – before the election of Mikhail Gorbachev to the leadership of the Communist Party (CPSU) in March 1985 inaugurated a new era of political stability, but one of economic and administrative change.

This Spotlight examines the important political, economic and foreign policy developments during this unsettled period. It looks at the changing power balances between the party and the state channels of government; the factional struggles between CPSU conservatives and policy reformers; the rise to power of the post-Stalin technocratic generation; the eastward and southward movement in the Soviet economy; the battle for economic reform; the collapse of détente and the commencement of a 'new cold war'; and the rise and subsequent repression of the dissident movement. It concludes with an analysis of the recent reform initiatives of the Gorbachev administration in the political, economic and cultural spheres in the wake of the February-March 1986 27th CPSU Congress and the post-Chernobyl drive for greater openness (glasnost).

THE REGIONS AND REPUBLICS OF THE SOVIET UNION

Part One

SOVIET POLITICAL ORGANISATION

The Soviet political system is marked by a stark divergence between its projected operation in theory and its practical functioning in reality. Marx and Lenin sought to replace what they saw as class-biased bourgeois democracy and Tsarist autocracy with a utopian order in which 'class distinctions have disappeared, . . . all production has been concentrated in the whole nation (and) the public power will lose its political character' (The Communist Manifesto). There would be a short interregnum period during which a 'Dictatorship of the Proletariat' would be imposed to sweep away lingering class enemies, before a truly egalitarian communist order would emerge and the state would 'wither away'. This stage had supposedly been reached by 1961 and yet Russia remains covered by a bewildering, interconnecting labyrinth of state and party apparatus controlling every aspect of life from the factory to the theatre. Presiding over this Byzantine bureaucracy are a new élite — the *apparatchiki* (full-time party officials).

On paper the Soviet Union is a federation of 15 republics (see Appendix A) with strong state (republic) institutions, universally elected state and federal committees and with a parallel supervisory party hierarchy and professional civil service. In reality, however, its Union Republics have only limited autonomous power (see Appendix A), the electoral system is bogus, and the real levers of power rest in the hands of the upper echelons of the Communist Party, who sit in the Politburo, the Central Committee, the Council of Ministers and the Secretariat and who move between key offices in the civil service, the army, industry and the police. Under Stalin, control of the political system became hyperconcentrated and autocratic with the consultative councils of the Politburo and the Central Committee falling into disuse. The period since Stalin's death (1953) has been

1

one of deconcentration, which has seen a revival in the functions of top level discussion committees, the corporatist co-option of a broader spectrum of interests — including leaders from industry and the military — on to these policy-making bodies, and a broadening of the ranks of Communist Party membership. It is no longer acceptable to view the Soviet system as one of iron diktat from above followed unswervingly by cowed officials and fervent party workers below. There exist, instead, clear policy and factional differences among the party hierarchy, with opportunities to block and delay implementation at intermediate levels. The most recent trends in such factional and policy conflicts at the apex of the Soviet system will be discussed in Parts Two and Four. First, however, a brief exposition of the organisational features and the evolution of this unique political system is given below.

The Elected State Soviet System

The Soviet political system can be viewed as consisting of three channels of communication and implementation between the decision-making executive and the public — an 'elected' state channel, a party channel and the civil service. Figure 1 outlines these routes and linkages.

The 'elected' tier of government is of value in legitimising and reaffirming the other channels of governance, but has limited independent power. It consists of over 45 000 *soviets* (people's councils) at the village, town, district, regional and republic levels, with, at the top, the *Supreme Soviet* — a two-chamber parliament serving the entire Soviet Union. These soviets comprise both party and non-party members with the party proportion increasing at each tier — from 40% in *oblast* (regional) soviets to 70% in the Supreme Soviet. All candidates for election need party approval and stand as 'joint candidates' with only one contestant permitted for each seat.[1] More than 2.3 million deputies man these soviets. The majority, who are carefully selected, dedicated and industrious representatives of the 'Soviet masses', carry out their duties part-time, receiving attendance

[1] In March 1979 a small group of dissidents 'Election 79', led by Vladimir Sichyov, attempted to put up two candidates (the historian Roy Medvedev and Ludmilla Agapora) against the official candidates in Moscow, but their applications were ruled invalid.

allowances and fringe benefits. A smaller core work full-time on the permanent committees at each level, and are invariably party members.

The local soviets are elected every two and a half years and meet in full session four to six times a year, delegating their day-to-day operations to a smaller, permanent party-dominated Executive Committee, and, at higher levels, to a smaller praesidium (in Soviet parlance a small and important executive committee) and to various functional departments. Thousands of 'Permanent Commissions' are also set up by soviets to check reactions in the localities to executive directives and to inspect local enterprises and institutions. The work of soviets — the bulk of which is routine and administrative, concerned with housing, health, education and transport — is supervised and controlled by Communist Party committees operating at the relevant level and by higher level Executive Committees, following the principles of 'democratic centralism' (see page 6). It is the party committees that propose the soviets' electoral slates.

Voting for these soviets is open to all adults and can formally be carried out in the privacy of a secluded booth. However, since the elector is presented with a form containing only one name and requiring no mark for approval, to vote in secret or to write on the ballot paper is taken as a sign of dissent and requires considerable courage. In such circumstances, nominated candidates find little difficulty in securing the necessary majority mandate in an election which, with an open register and great state efforts to secure full voting, invariably records turnouts in excess of 99%.[1]

The Supreme Soviet, which rests at the apex of the state pyramid, is in theory the chief legislative authority in the Russian political system, but in practice it is merely a rubber stamp for laws presented to it.

The lower chamber of the Supreme Soviet (Soviet of the Union) is elected every five years by the people in the proportion of one deputy to each 350 000 voters: the upper chamber (Soviet of the Nationalities) is composed of deputies from the republics and regions (see Appendix A and Appendix D). In all there are 1500 deputies, a third of whom are party functionaries, government

---

[1] In the most recent March 1984 Supreme Soviet elections the turnout recorded was 99.9% and only 0.05% of voters, 100 000, registered a vote against the candidate presented.

3

FIGURE 1: THE POLITICAL STRUCTURE OF THE USSR

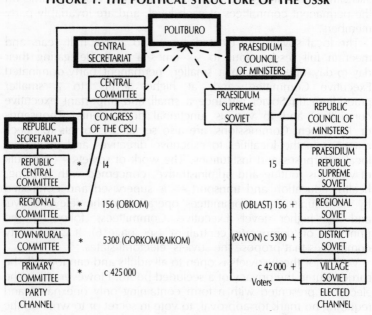

NOTES: Thick rimmed boxes denotes full-time official bodies. Each committee marked with an * is appointed by a biennial congress, and in turn appoints its own small, full-time bureau and secretariat. Each Soviet marked with a + 'elects' in addition its own Executive Committee.

ministers or top ranking military and police officers; the remainder consist of a select and representative mix of the various professions, social classes, nationalities, sexes and age groups of the Soviet Union following an unwritten quota system. The turnover rate for members at successive Supreme Soviets is high — sometimes exceeding 60%. This allows wide numbers of loyal citizens to be rewarded and an impression of mass representation and control over public affairs to be illusorily created.

This huge assembly meets for brief, three or four day sessions twice a year. Besides unanimously approving and ratifying important legislation, it also 'elects' (though the nomination slate is, in fact, drawn up by the Communist Party hierarchy), a number of administrative bodies. One is a Praesidium of 39 members (including the chairmen of the 15 republic Supreme Soviets, and key Communist Party Politburo and Central Committee functionaries) to act for the Supreme Soviet when it is out of session (see Appendix C). It also 'elects' a Council of Ministers which is formally the supreme administrative organ of the USSR. Numerous specific and permanent Commissions are also constituted to meet quarterly and examine policy proposals, under the Praesidium's direction. These Commissions, which in total might contain nearly three-quarters of the Supreme Soviet's deputies, are bodies of significance, but are dominated by high ranking officials (oblast secretaries and Central Committee candidates), with the proportion of ordinary workers and peasants far below that to be found in the wider assembly. For these delegates, membership of the Supreme Soviet is largely honorific; his or her duty is to propagandise and further the support for pronounced policies at the constituency level and to act as a 'status model' for the public below.

With the 1977 Constitution defining the USSR as a 'parliamentarian republic', the elected state channel is legally recognised as the mainspring of authority in the Soviet Union. Thus, the chairman of the Praesidium should formally be viewed as the nation's president or head of state and the chairman of the Council of Ministers as its prime minister (see Appendix E). The Council of Ministers is certainly a key centre of power at the apex of the Soviet political system (see page 9). It is, however, the Communist Party, led by its General Secretary and Politburo, which directs and integrates the various levels and channels of government and wields ultimate power in the Soviet Union.

The Party Machine

At the centre of the second and most significant channel of administration and communication is the Communist Party of the Soviet Union (CPSU), which, through Article 6 of the Constitution, has been guaranteed a monopoly position in a one-party state. During the years preceding and following the October 1917 Revolution, the party functioned for Lenin as a revolutionary and enlightened 'vanguard of the proletariat' in a backward, traditionalist nation where the material conditions for communism were unfavourable and which teemed with hostile counter-revolutionary forces. In such circumstances a premium was placed upon unity and discipline and obedience to orders from above. To achieve this, Lenin developed the unique organising principle for the Communist Party and for Soviet government in general — 'democratic centralism'. This concept allows for, in theory, free political discussion and the election of officers from below in a pyramidically organised party structure. Its key tenet is, however, the disciplined compliance with, and execution of, decisions 'democratically' agreed to and the unconditional subordination of all lower organs to those above.

During the early 1920s, when the Communist Party was composed of a comparatively small group of committed ideologues, the tail of the movement was allowed to exert considerable influence. But as strong policy differences and groupings emerged, as party membership broadened and as Josef Stalin strengthened his hold, centralist principles triumphed over democratic ones and power became increasingly concentrated at the apex of the party structure. Instead of committees below electing representatives to higher committees, the channel of selection was reversed with secretaries and officers being vetted and appointed from above. Tremendous patronage power was created at the upper levels of the party apparatus enabling small empires to be carved out by individual leaders. Under Stalin, with his secret police, personnel purges and 'special department' henchmen, such concentration of power was taken to its autocratic extreme.

Stalin's successor Nikita Khrushchev sought to revive the 'Leninist democracy' of the 1920s and make the party a more responsive and efficient machine for effecting advances in the Soviet economy. Under Khrushchev one-man dictatorship was replaced by collective leadership through the revived Politburo and by drawing upon the broader Central Committee for advice and endorsement. Technicians and experts from economic and scientific fields were to be drawn into consultations; the power and independence of the secret police was to be curbed as the new KGB was brought under closer party control; and, thirdly, party membership was to be further expanded to form a loyal, efficient and more populist executive arm to ensure that decisions from above were properly implemented. In 1961, under new Rule Number 25, Khrushchev went even further and attempted to shake up the lower and intermediate secretarial ranks of the party machine and prevent the formation of ossified patronage networks and cliques through the statutory retirement of a significant proportion of officials after each election.

These reforms moved the Soviet state away from the worse excesses of Stalinism with its crowded *gulags* (enforced labour camps) and cowed populace and officials. Membership of the Communist Party — the 'civic army' into which appropriate citizens are sponsored and co-opted — expanded from barely 6 million in 1953 (3.3% of the total population) to over 10 million in 1964 (4.6% of the total population). Wider, although still limited, discussion of policy alternatives was now seen and new shifting coalitions emerged. Khrushchev was, however, ousted in October 1964 by the more conservative troika of Brezhnev, Kosygin and Podgorny and a number of his more radical departures, including Rule 25 and his decentralist economic reforms, were repealed. The basic features of the Khrushchev party structure have, however, remained in place and the growth in party membership, transforming the CPSU into a mass party embracing intellectuals, blue-collar, white-collar and rural workers, has continued. Thus by 1984 CPSU membership stood at 18.4 million[1] (6.7% of the total population and 9.3% of the adult population), with another 1.5 million being attached to the Komsomol (Young Communist Youth League for those under the age of 28), and its organisation had assumed a mature, settled and structured form.

At the base of the party hierarchy (see Figure 1) rest the more than 425 000 Primary Party Units (PPUs) which are established at any workplace — factory, collective farm, office, shop — where more than three party members are employed. The organisational form a PPU takes varies with the membership of each unit — a small PPU elects only a part-time secretary, those with over 15 members (there were more than 255 000 such PPUs in 1983) elect a committee and bureau, while those with more than 150 members (approximately 25 000 of the total in 1983) are entitled to a full-time salaried official. The PPU holds monthly general meetings, sees that its enterprise is running properly and meeting its targets, and ensures that instructions from above are implemented. The committees and bureaux are the important

---

[1] 44.4% of CPSU members were classed as 'workers', 12.2% as collective farmers and 43.4% as technical intelligentsia, administrators, servicemen and professionals. 59.7% were 'Great Russians' and 27.9% were women. 0.7 million of this total were 'candidate members' still on probation.

bodies at this level, with over two million members serving in them. Such members include responsible factory directors and chief engineers and an inner core of 'permanent activists'.

Above the PPUs, which have been steadily increasing in numbers and size since the 1950s, lie the biennial district, town and urban conferences to which PPUs send delegates and which elect the district party committee (the *raikom*) and its secretariat and bureau, each of which is responsible for 150 to 200 PPUs. Similarly organised above this level rest the 156 regional (oblast) conferences with their regional committees (*obkom*); above these lie the 14 Republic Congresses and Committees, and at the apex of the party structure there is the quinquennial All-Union Congress which 'elects' the Central Committee, the Politburo and the Secretariat.

Several features distinguish this party hierarchy. First, as one ascends the pyramid of congresses and committees so the machine structure becomes more professional (staffed with party apparatchiks who dominate the obkom level and above) and differentiated. At obkom level there are individual secretaries with responsibility for industry, agriculture, ideological work, etc., supervising and working in connection with the state authorities on the corresponding level. Secondly, it is with the bureaux and secretaryships that day-to-day authority and control resides. These bodies are hierarchically inter-connected and staffed by full-time white-collar officials, who slowly work their way up to oblast level or above. They form a party apparatchik élite of less than one million. Thirdly, officials and activists from lower organisations can sit simultaneously on different bodies within the party hierarchy. Fourthly, and most importantly, each level in the hierarchy is responsible for the performance and personnel of the body below it. Thus 'elections' of officials are in reality vetted appointments supervised from above (the *nomenklatura* system) ensuring obedience, loyalty and conformity: conferring considerable powers of patronage to secretaries at successive levels. It is at the highest levels in the Politburo and Secretariat that ultimate and most extensive power and patronage reside. Thus with each change in leadership there are considerable changes in personnel at the highest levels, as the supporters of the new power brokers are promoted to prominent positions. Such transmutations feed through in due course to the ranks below.

The Loci of Power

The totalitarian Soviet political system differs in obvious and basic respects from the Western 'liberal democracy' model with its freedom of elections and press, its party plurality, its interest group autonomy, and its separation of judicial, executive and legislative powers. Instead of the pluralistic democracy of the West, which for Marxists merely created dominance by one class over another, the Soviet model has been deliberately monistic with the Communist Party co-ordinating and ensuring classless rule in accordance with Marxist-Leninist principles. It is for this reason that party cadres are to be found in commanding positions in all professions and institutions — in the soviets, the army, judiciary, police (where over 95% are party members), civil service, media, education, industry and in collective-farm management. Party membership provides a key route to the top, and is in many respects a condition of service in superior grade posts.

Such a cross-cutting and interlocking web of personnel and interests is the key characteristic of Russian policy-making and executive structures at the apex of the party and state hierarchies. The Praesidium of the Supreme Soviet and the Council of Ministers are the key advisory bodies at the head of the 'elected' state system: the Central Committee of the Party Congress and the Central Secretariat are even more powerful bodies which direct the party machine. The Politburo is the hub around which all these bodies revolve (see Figure 2) and the prime source of political power in the Soviet Union. Mention has already been made of the Praesidium of the Supreme Soviet, the least influential of these five bodies: attention will thus be focused here upon the other four formations.

Council of Ministers (COM) This body comprises over 130 members and includes the ministerial heads of the different departments of the civil service and state industrial and administrative machine, the head of the KGB and State Bank, the chairmen of important specialist government committees and commissions and the chairmen of the 15 Union Republic Councils of Ministers. These top-ranking government ministers are also members of the CPSU Central Committee and are in charge of overseeing the implementation of economic programmes and the maintenance of law and order. The COM is thus an important body and is the main source of government

FIGURE 2: PARTY AND GOVERNMENTAL INTERCONNECTIONS

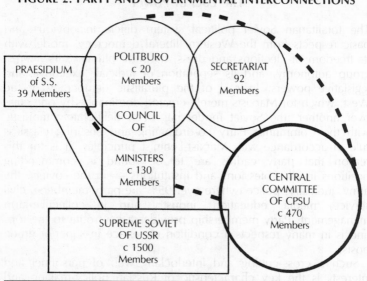

legislation, meeting twice a year to issue decrees and regulations in the economic and social spheres. A smaller Praesidium of the COM, composed of a (prime minister) chairman, three first deputy chairmen and eight deputy chairmen (including the head of the Gosplan State Planning Committee), meets weekly to co-ordinate activities and to balance out rival claims for resources between different departments and republics. It operates as an 'economic cabinet' and liaises closely with the CPSU Politburo, with which body there is an overlap of personnel.

Party Congress The Party Congress is a large forum at which over 5000 delegates gather every five years, coinciding with each Five Year Plan, to enthusiastically receive and endorse new policy directives.[1] Of these delegates, 2000 consist of top party functionaries and government officials, distinguished scientists

---

[1] The first Congress of the CPSU (then known as the Russian Social Democratic Labour Party) was held in March 1898 and proceeded to meet in regular annual or biennial sessions in the years up to 1934. Between 1935 and 1953, however, only three Congresses were held. Since 1961, Congresses have been held quinquenially, meeting in October 1961 (22nd), March 1966 (23rd), March 1971 (24th), February 1976 (25th), February 1981 (26th) and February 1986 (27th).

and scholars, and high ranking military officers. The remainder form a hand-picked selection of rank and file party members, with great attention being paid to due representation by age, sex and ethnic groups. The activities of the Congress, which lasts for a week, take place with great media publicity and before a coterie of guests from sympathetic foreign communist parties. As in the Supreme Soviet however, following the principles of 'democratic centralism', Congress delegates have no real power. Their job is to acclaim the speeches delivered by party dignitaries, to ratify each proposal presented and to accept the new slate of members for the Central Committee, which has been prepared beforehand.

Central Committee of the CPSU   It is here that real authority can first be perceived. This Committee is composed of around 300 full voting members and 170 non voting 'candidates' whose official task is to lead the party during the period between quinquennial Congresses and meet twice a year in closed session. It represents a grand consultative council with seats on it reserved for: secretaries from the Secretariat, the first secretaries of the 14 Republican parties and the Moscow and Leningrad parties, obkomy party secretaries (who make up a third of its membership), key ministers and members of the Council of Ministers, officials from the KGB and the military, chairmen and secretaries from the trade unions and the Komsomol youth organisation, and occasional representatives from industries, collectives, education and science. It represents the party and bureaucratic élite and is elderly (with an average age of around 60), male and predominantly Russian. Membership of the Central Committee is regulated by the Politburo and Secretariat and forms a key rung — first as candidate and then as a full member — on the slow ladder upwards to the Politburo and the very top. The rate of turnover of Central Committee members only accelerates during periods of leadership change within the latter body.[1]

Khrushchev used the Central Committee as a sounding board and publicity body for new policy proposals in agriculture and

---

[1] The survival rates for existing Central Committee members at successive quinquennial party congresses have been: 1956 — 62%; 1961 — 50%, 1966 — 79%; 1971 — 76%; 1976 — 83%; 1986 — 60%. During this same period, to maintain upward mobility, the number of full members in the Central Committee more than doubled from 133 in 1956 to 307 in 1986.

industry, promoting his supporters on to the council. This support he used in 1957, when a conservative 'anti-party' faction led by Malenkov and Molotov gained a Politburo majority against Khrushchev's decentralisation proposals. Khrushchev went back to the Central Committee and received an endorsement enabling him to remove the opposition faction from the Politburo. Such a use of the Central Committee has, however, been unusual. During the following two decades, under Brezhnev, the Central Committee was used less as a consultative forum and more as a select gathering to which results and new policies were reported.

The Politburo and Secretariat It is the Politburo which since 1953 has been the chief source of power in the Soviet political system, with the Secretariat functioning as its operational arm and vigilant, supervisory eyes. It is here that the key 'party bosses' vie for control and dominance.

The *Politburo* is 'elected' by the Central Committee and comprises between 10 and 15 voting members and a smaller number of 'candidates' and meets weekly behind closed doors. Its leader, and the *de facto* head of the Soviet Union, is the CPSU General Secretary and the rest of the Politburo is nowadays composed of leading party officials (from within the Secretariat), ministers (including Defence and Foreign Affairs from the COM), the chairmen of the KGB and Party Control Commission, First Secretaries of the party from the major cities (Moscow and Leningrad) and regions (for example, the Ukraine), the President of the Supreme Soviet and chairmen from the Council of Ministers. This has followed the decision in 1973 by Leonid Brezhnev to bring in representatives of all the main centres of Soviet power — Gromyko from the Foreign Ministry, Andropov from the KGB, Marshal Grechko from the armed forces — so that an eye could be kept on serious rivals. The Politburo functions as a political cabinet and is concerned with framing broad economic and ideological goals for the nation and with foreign and defence policy. Leadership of this key body has shifted between the collective, personal and factional — depending upon the authority, personality and policy successes of the General Secretary in charge.

The *Secretariat* is the administrative support or 'general staff' to the Politburo and is composed of Secretaries at the head of various functional departments staffed by full-time party civil servants. A third to a half of its twelve members usually serve on the Politburo at the same time. It works in conjunction with Ministries — in charge of the day-to-day running of their services — to ensure proper functioning and provisioning; it prepares drafts and provides information required by the Politburo and Central Committee. The Secretariat also sends instructions to lower level party bodies and it controls and proposes appointments for significant posts within the party organisation, the armed forces, the ministries, the press, the trade unions, education and at embassies overseas. It functions full-time but meets weekly as a body for discussions which are chaired by the CPSU General Secretary and which are addressed by industrial, academic and scientific experts on an ad hoc basis.

It is clear from the above that the premier institutions in the Soviet Union work together in a convoluted and arcane fashion, with personnel constantly changing hats as they move from committee to committee.[1] The general rule is one of dominance of councils by bodies above and of the state channel by the party. It is the Communist Party, with its historic 'guiding role' prescribed in the constitution, which co-ordinates all activities through its core of less than one million apparatchiks. These key party members are drawn from a mixture of manual, peasant and professional backgrounds, but commonly boast high standards of technical education and enjoy significant economic and social privileges. They are involved in a broad range of party, state and extra-governmental activities and monopolise the key posts in Soviet society. Vetted and appointed from above, they represent a self-perpetuating and almost Confucian élite.

However, although it is the Politburo-Secretariat, with its members also involved in the state structure in the Council of Ministers and Praesidium of the Supreme Soviet, which dominates the political system, it operates under constraints from 'institutional interest groups' located at the republic and obkom level of the party and within the heavy industries, police, agriculture, light industries and the armed forces. Leaders of these interest groups bargain inside the Council of Ministers and

---

[1]   In February 1987, for example, of the eleven full and eight candidate members of the CPSU Politburo, seven served in the Praesidium of the Supreme Soviet (Gromyko, its chairman, Gorbachev, Shcherbitsky, Slyunkov, Yeltsin, Solovyov and Demichev), seven in the Council of Ministers (Ryzhkov, its chairman, Aliyev, Vorotnikov, Chebrikov, Sokolov, Shevardnadze and Talyzin) and six in the Secretariat (Gorbachev, Ligachev, Zaikov, Dolgikh, Slyunkov and Yakovlev).

CPSU Central Committee, and ultimately within the Politburo. The balance of power within and between these apical bodies is potentially fluid, with much depending upon the strength and unity of the leadership around the General Secretary. The realities of the Soviet economy and society today also impose boundaries and limitations upon change. The following pages examine these realities and look at the political and policy changes of the last decade.

Part Two

POLITICAL CHANGES

The Background to the Brezhnev Era

Lenin, Stalin and Khrushchev: From Revolution to Rejection, 1917-1964

The first half century of communist rule in the Soviet Union was dominated by the three sharply contrasting figures of Vladimir Lenin, Josef Stalin and Nikita Khrushchev. It began amid a wave of optimistic revolutionary fervour, but ended with the ignominious removal of the incumbent CPSU leader by his most senior colleagues. For more than 30 of the intervening years control of the party was engrossed by a tyrannical despot who radically restructured and distorted the Soviet economic and political system.

Vladimir Lenin (1870-1924), the 'Great Russian' son of an affluent white-collar educational inspector from Simbirsk (Ulyanovsk), created the Bolshevik Party (renamed the CPSU in 1917) with its disciplined, 'democratic centralist' form of organisation. He then took full advantage of the disturbed and anarchic conditions of 1917 and manoeuvred the party into power in the 'revolutionary coup' of October 1917. During the next seven years, working in combination with the Red Army leader Leon Trotsky, Lenin ensured the survival of the new regime during the 'Civil War' of 1917-21, established a new and lasting framework for government and reinvigorated the shattered Soviet economy with the introduction of the pragmatic, mixed economy *New Economic Policy (NEP)* of 1921-27.

Lenin's successor as *de facto* ruler of the Soviet Union, Josef Stalin (1879-1953), was a far more ruthless, dogmatic and autocratic personality. Born the son of a poor Georgian

15

cobbler-serf, Stalin lacked the intellectual refinement of Lenin and made his reputation less through force of argument or charisma, but more through his organisational ability and steel. He became party manager in 1919 and General Secretary in 1922 and used this power base in the years between 1924 and 1929 to ease aside his rivals Bukharin, Zinoviev, Kamenev and Trotsky and emerge as the controlling force in the Soviet polity. He then proceeded to abandon the pragmatic, quasi-capitalist New Economic Policy and institute a radical programme of agricultural collectivisation and heavy industrialisation in an effort to fundamentally rearrange the Soviet economic and social base, and by so doing rapidly transform the nation from an agrarian to a top-ranking industrial power and so construct the world's first truly socialist state.

Stalin's programme of 'socialism in one country' proved in a number of respects to be remarkably successful. For example, during the years between 1929 and 1940 Soviet industry grew at an unprecedented average rate of 16% per annum, the blue-collar labour force quadrupled in size and the country's urban population doubled. By the 1940s a large new and modern heavy industry base had been constructed, a major social transfiguration had been effected in which the vestigial feudal and capitalist elements had been expunged and the influence of the CPSU had been spread into rural areas and been strengthened through educational indoctrination and through major new 'worker-technician' recruitment drives. The social and political cost of this transformation was, however, appalling, with the stress being placed upon ends rather than means. In the rural sector, millions of 'rich peasant' *kulaks* were liquidated or sent to labour camps in Siberia, agricultural produce was forcibly marketed and per capita living standards reduced, as the countryside was squeezed to provide investment income for heavy industrialisation. Politically, the balanced Leninist party-state political system was cruelly disfigured by the paranoid and autocratic Stalin. Inner party democracy and morale was shattered by a series of horrendous 'purges' of old guard opponents, which reached a peak in 1936-38 with the executions of Kamenev, Zinoviev and Bukharin, and by the personalised manner of Stalin's rule. He governed through his own 'special department' and was assisted by the secret police under the control of his Georgian crony Lavrenti Beria, whose brutal and intrusive tactics served to create a climate of terror which

16

ensured the cowed loyalty and obedience of party and state bureaucrats.

The Stalinist transformation was, however, not based upon force and terror alone. It gained the support of many of the new generation of socialist-educated 'worker-bureaucrats' who benefited from the opportunities for the rapid upward social mobility which was presented during these years. It also gained the tacit support of urban workers and the military, who were the chief beneficiaries of 'forced industrialisation'. Stalin was thirdly able to make use of the nation's Tsarist political tradition of respect for strong, centralised and symbolic leadership, as well as drawing upon the deep roots of Slavic nationalism. The latter became most clear during the 'Great Patriotic War' of 1941-45, during which the Soviet people rallied behind the communist government to ward off the anti-Slavic Nazi invaders.

Stalin was succeeded, after his death in March 1953, by a 'collective leadership' of his leading servants from the state (Malenkov, Molotov, Bulganin and Kaganovich), party (Khrushchev), military (Zhukov) and police (Beria) machines. However, despite such close links with Stalin, there was a consensus among these figures, with the one notable exception of secret police chief Beria, that fundamental changes needed to be made to the Stalinist system and style of government in the ensuing era. Rule by terror needed to be abandoned and replaced by one based upon popular respect and incentives; the balanced Leninist party-state political system needed to be rekindled and regularised; citizens should be given rights in the civil sphere and made aware of the limits for political opposition and dissent; and changes needed to be made to the Soviet economic system to remedy the inherited evils of overbureaucratisation and low productivity and to give greater emphasis to the consumer sectors of agriculture and light industry.

In pursuance of these aims, the state, party and military leaders immediately joined ranks to remove from power Lavrenti Beria (who was tried and executed in December 1953) and reorganise the secret police, bringing it under firm party control. A liberalising 'thaw' in the cultural and intellectual climate was immediately seen and was buttressed by the renewed functioning of top-level state and party consultative and discussion bodies, the reactivation of trade unions and soviets and the promulgation of a new legal code.

17

However, while the post-Stalin state and party leaders were in broad agreement over the need to humanise, popularise and legitimise the Soviet political system, significant differences existed over emphases as well as priorities in the economic sphere. The state bureaucracy leader, Georgiy Malenkov (1902-), favoured retaining significant power within the state government machine and was an advocate of giving greater investment priority to the agricultural and light industry sectors at the expense of the heavy industry-military complex. The party leader, Nikita Khrushchev (1894-1971), sought, by contrast, to assert the firmer control of a cleansed and reinvigorated CPSU over the Soviet polity and economy and was anxious to maintain high investment in the heavy industry-defence sector. He aimed to raise agricultural and light industrial production through organisational reform rather than through rechannelling investment.

During the years between 1954 and 1957 a fierce and personalised struggle thus developed between Malenkov and Khrushchev for effective control of the Soviet polity. It was Khrushchev, the forceful peasant's son from Kursk, who emerged the victor. His policy package appeared, on the surface, to be more moderate and less disruptive of traditional practices than that presented by Malenkov, thus appealing to the influential military and heavy industry lobbies. This, allied with support from within the party machine, enabled Khrushchev to dislodge the state bureaucracy trio of Malenkov, Molotov (1890-1986) and Kaganovich (1893-) at the infamous Central Committee plenum of June 1957 and to remove Bulganin (1895-1975) a year later. In contrast with the Stalin era, however, the lives of these 'purged' opponents were spared, with each being granted administrative posts in the remote regions of the Urals, East Kazakhstan and Mongolia.

With his state government rivals ousted, Khrushchev emerged as the supremely dominant force in Soviet politics between 1957 and 1964 and proceeded to implement a series of reforms aimed at 'de-Stalinising' Soviet society, modernising and raising the efficiency of the Soviet economy and establishing the pre-eminence of the CPSU over all other state bodies. In the implementation of this programme Khrushchev proceeded to go much further than his early supporters had expected and he began to encounter, in consequence, a rising level of opposition. He was an arrogant, assertive and impulsive leader who sought grand solutions and instant results and who disliked the pettifogging interference of cautious bureaucrats. He became committed, through the Ten Year Plan and new Party Programme of 1959 and 1961, to the precipitate modernisation of the Soviet economy and the rapid attainment of 'full communism', pledging the nation to a 'race with the West' in the economic, military and political spheres. He proved, however, to be an erratic and inconsistent leader, suddenly switching policy tack over key issues such as improved relations with the West, cultural liberalisation and the priority to be given to the agricultural-consumer goods sector *vis-à-vis* heavy industry and defence.

In the economic, military and political spheres the Khrushchev years were characterised by the introduction of a number of novel and grandiose policy programmes and by an inveterate recourse to institutional reorganisation. For example, schemes were introduced to open up millions of hectares of 'virgin land' in Kazakhstan, to extend the cultivation of maize, to boost the production of chemical fertilisers and to expand and modernise the nation's nuclear rocket forces. In the state sphere, regional economic councils (*sovnarkhozy*) were established to replace the old central industrial ministries in 1956 as well as new co-ordinating Agricultural Boards. In the party sphere, the controversial democratising Rule 25 was introduced, district (*rayon*) committees were abolished and oblast and republican party committees divided into separate and specialised agricultural and industrial hierarchies. In the cultural sphere, periodic liberalising 'thaws' were launched in 1953-54, 1956-57 and 1961-62 and Stalinism roundly condemned in Khrushchev's 'secret speech' in February 1956. Overseas, Khrushchev sought to promote a new policy of 'peaceful co-existence' with the West, but found himself frustrated by the Berlin dispute of 1961 and the Cuban missile crisis of 1962.

The balance sheet of the Khrushchev reform programme proved to be mixed. Initially, it gave a beneficial boost to the Soviet economy and society but it had a destabilising impact abroad, precipitating anti-Stalinist revolts in Poland, Czechoslovakia, East Germany and Hungary in 1956 and leading to a rift in relations between China and the Soviet Union. From 1960, however, Khrushchev began to encounter increasing problems with the domestic economy as a result of harvest failures and overcropping in Kazakhstan. He responded to this, partly prompted by the outbreak of workers' riots in a number of Soviet cities in 1960, by giving renewed emphasis to reform in the years between 1962 and 1964 and by shifting resources away from defence towards agriculture and light industry in a Malenkovian manner.[1] This strategy, however, undermined the coalition of heavy industry, military and state support which had maintained Khrushchev in power between 1956-60 and created the conditions for Khrushchev's removal in 1964.

The ousting of Khrushchev as CPSU General Secretary in October 1964 was a dramatic event for contemporary observers. In retrospect, however, it was by no means surprising. Khrushchev had alienated influential élite groups within the Soviet polity — the state government bureaucracy, district and regional party leaders, and heavy industry and military chiefs — as a result of policies and reforms introduced between 1956 and 1963. In addition, Khrushchev's abrasive personality and his increasingly personalised and domineering style of rule caused growing friction among his most senior colleagues. As early as 1958 Khrushchev had combined the two posts of party General Secretary and state leader (prime minister). In the succeeding six years he abandoned the principle of 'collective rule' and governed in a presidentialist and populist fashion, impulsively making policies from the hip, berating his party and state bureaucrat colleagues in televised and published speeches, reshuffling personnel at whim and engaging in incessant 'meet the people' tours across the Soviet Union.

The emergence of intra-party élite opposition to Khrushchev's style of rule was first made clear at the Central Committee plenum of May 1960, when an influential group led by Mikhail Suslov, the CPSU's ultra-conservative ideologist who was committed to rapprochement with Communist China, and Frol Kozlov, the former Leningrad party leader who had close ties with the heavy industry-military lobby, forced a number of policy and personnel changes on the General Secretary. This opposition gained strength in 1962 and 1963, as a result of a widening dissatisfaction with Khrushchev's party reforms, his new defence programme and his renewed 'de-Stalinisation' drive. It reached a peak in 1964, following a disastrous double harvest failure in the Ukraine and Kazakhstan. Khrushchev, aware of this mounting

---

[1] Khrushchev announced plans in 1960 to reduce army ground-force manpower by 1.2 million men, including 250 000 career officers.

dissent in élite ranks, laid plans to effect a pre-emptive purge of the CPSU Secretariat and Politburo in the winter of 1964. This served, however, only to unite his opponents, who acted first themselves. At a carefully organised Central Committee plenum on 14 October 1964, Mikhail Suslov read out a list of charges indicting Khrushchev's leadership record, proposed the party leader's resignation on the grounds of 'advanced age' and 'deteriorating health' and nominated Leonid Brezhnev as the new CPSU General Secretary. The motion was carried by an overwhelming majority. A day later Khrushchev was compelled to resign his state premiership, being replaced by Alexei Kosygin. He retired to a secluded *dacha* for the final seven years of his life and became a forgotten 'unperson' in the history of Soviet communism.

Conservatism and Consolidation: The Brezhnev Era, 1964-1982

Nikita Khrushchev was succeeded by a new 'collective leadership' based around the figures of Leonid Brezhnev, Alexei Kosygin, Mikhail Suslov, Nikolai Podgorny and Alexander Shelepin and in which a clear attempt was made to maintain a personnel division between the party and state spheres of government. This 'collectivist' style of governing and separation between party and state channels was to endure on paper for the next 18 years. In reality, however, one man, Leonid Brezhnev, was to progressively emerge as the dominant and controlling force in Soviet politics in the years after 1964.

Had it not been for the incapacitating stroke suffered by the influential Frol Kozlov in April 1963, Brezhnev would probably not have ascended to the rank of CPSU party leader in October 1964. However, with Kozlov immobilised, he formed a safe, centrist and obvious compromise choice to replace Khrushchev.[1] Brezhnev had enjoyed a lengthy and wide-ranging career which had enabled him to build up influential connections not only within the central party machine, but also in the provinces and within military, heavy industry, agricultural and diplomatic leadership cadres. During his apprenticeship period he had developed a reputation for pragmatism, flexible

---

[1] Kozlov subsequently died in February 1965.

21

orthodoxy, efficiency, loyalty and calmness. These were qualities which appealed to the post-Khrushchev leadership circle who wished to pursue a cautious, moderate and consensual policy programme which would mix selected elements of Stalinism and Khrushchevism in a conservative, utilitarian fashion.

Brezhnev's Apprenticeship for Power: 1906-1964

Brezhnev was representative of the new generation of Stalinist 'worker-technicians' who rapidly ascended the party hierarchy as a result of the inter-war purges of old-guard communists and who provided political leadership during the 1941-45 'Great Patriotic War'. His career before becoming CPSU General Secretary in 1964 provides an interesting case study of the means of climbing the party ladder and the vital importance of patronage connections in post-war and contemporary Soviet polity.

Born in December 1906 in the small, but growing, town of Dneprodzerzhinsk in the Ukraine, Leonid Ilyich Brezhnev was the first Soviet leader to be drawn from true proletarian stock. His father was a 'Great Russian' steelworker from Kursk (Khrushchev's native region) in Central Russia, who had migrated to the industrialising Ukraine during the final decade of the 19th century. Leonid was brought up during a period of turmoil and shortages, his secondary education at the local factory school being interrupted by the revolution and civil war of 1917-21, and developed from this experience an innate instinct for adaptation and survival. When his family moved back to Kursk in 1923 he became involved in politics and joined the Komsomol, partly as a means of enhancing his future job prospects. Under Komsomol instruction and guidance Brezhnev was trained as an agricultural surveyor and worked on the collectivisation programmes in Byelorussia and at Sverdlovsk in the Urals during the later 1920s. Then in 1931, after being accepted into full membership of the CPSU, he was assigned back to his native Dneprodzerzhinsk to retrain as an industrial engineer, before being appointed head of the new local Metallurgical Polytechnic.

Brezhnev's career within the party first began in earnest, however, in 1938 when Nikita Khrushchev arrived from Moscow with a brief from his master Stalin to thoroughly purge the old, independent-minded, leadership of the local Ukrainian Communist Party and bring in a new and more loyal generation of personnel. Brezhnev was thus catapulted to the post of party secretary in charge of propaganda at the oblast capital of Dnepropetrovsk and proceeded to work closely with Khrushchev during the latter's stay as Ukrainian Party First Secretary between 1938 and 1947. He impressed Khrushchev with his energy, organisational ability and loyalty and his facility to adapt adroitly to each new change in official policy line. Brezhnev's ascent up the ranks of the local Ukrainian Communist Party thus proved to be rapid. He served as a Political Commissar to the local Southern Army between 1941-45 and, following a further purge, he served as local oblast chief between 1946 and 1949. Here, involving himself fully in post-war rural and industrial reconstruction work, he found his true niche. He also during these years began to develop his own network of local personal contacts from within party, industrial and military ranks — the so-called 'Dnieper mafia' — which were to endure and be drawn upon in the years after 1964.

It was, however, Brezhnev's own clientship connection with the rising figure of Nikita Khrushchev which was to be more important in 1950. Khrushchev, who had been transferred back to Moscow, drafted in Brezhnev to serve temporarily in the agricultural department of the CPSU Central Committee, before arranging his reassignment to Moldavia, where he was to take charge as the new party leader. This appointment, involving control of a Republic, represented a considerable promotion and brought Brezhnev under the direct gaze of the party leader Josef Stalin. It was a difficult and demanding posting, Brezhnev taking over a recently purged local party machine and being instructed to fully 'Sovietise' and establish CPSU authority within a republic which had only recently been ceded from Romania. He adapted quickly to the needs of the situation and, diligently following orders, proceeded brutally to liquidate the local kulak community, expunge internal opposition and rapidly introduce collectivised agriculture on the Soviet model.

Such resolution impressed Josef Stalin who inducted Brezhnev into the CPSU Central Committee and Secretariat and appointed him a 'candidate' member of the Politburo at the 19th Party Congress in October 1952. Brezhnev proceeded to join Stalin's 'inner circle' of closest advisers in 1952-53 and but for the party leader's death in March 1953 would have entered the

Politburo as one of its leading members in 1954. Instead, however, he was to suffer from the immediate 'de-Stalinist' reaction which followed the General Secretary's death on 5 March 1953, losing both his Secretariat and Politburo 'candidate' seats within the space of 48 hours. Brezhnev rapidly rebounded from this setback, however, as a result of his close relations with the ascendant Khrushchev. In 1954 he was sent to Kazakhstan to take charge of Khrushchev's important new 'Virgin Lands' agricultural programme and, after a successful two years, he returned to Moscow in February 1956 to be re-elected as a 'candidate' member of the Politburo and reinducted into the powerful Secretariat. His task in this body was to liaise with overseas communist parties and to oversee the co-ordination of the Soviet Union's new space and nuclear missile programme. A year later Brezhnev was promoted to full membership of the Politburo at the infamous Central Committee plenum of June 1957 and appointed to the additional patronage-wielding post of deputy chairman of the bureau in charge of the CPSU within the Russian Federation.

During the years between 1957 and 1960, with Khrushchev at the height of his power, Leonid Brezhnev served as one of the party leader's closest and most influential troubleshooting advisers. He was to endure, however, a reverse in his fortunes in May 1960 when Khrushchev's authority began to be challenged by the duumvirate of Suslov and Kozlov, being removed from the Politburo and Secretariat and despatched 'upstairs' to the largely ceremonial post of State President. He showed typical resiliency, however, and made full use of his new position to maintain a high public profile, meeting the numerous visiting dignitaries, engaging in frequent diplomatic missions and establishing for himself a new reputation as an effective international statesman. Brezhnev also during this period (1960-64), aware of the direction in which the political tide was slowly turning, began to gradually distance himself from his patron Khrushchev and voice public disagreement over a number of his new policy approaches. In particular, he made clear his differences over three contemporary issues: the priority that was beginning to be given to the consumer sector *vis-à-vis* heavy industry and defence; the plans to rely increasingly in the future on nuclear defence to the detriment of conventional ground-force numbers; and the withdrawal of troops from East Germany and the handling of the 1962 Berlin crisis. On all three issues, Brezhnev adopted a more conservative and hawkish stance than the incumbent Khrushchev.

This change in policy stance proved to be of benefit to Brezhnev in the 1963-64 succession struggle. He was able to emerge as an attractive centre-right alternative to party-leader Khrushchev and be adopted as heir-apparent by the 'kingmaking' Mikhail Suslov following Frol Kozlov's cerebral stroke in April 1963. With this new support, Brezhnev stepped down as State President in July 1964 and was re-elected to the Secretariat as its second ranking member. Three months later, on 14 October 1964, he was chosen as the new party General Secretary to replace the ousted Khrushchev. His calm, composed, consensual personality, his wide-ranging intra-party and intra-élite connections, and his cautious conservatism on many key issues made him the obvious choice for a Central Committee seeking a period of tranquility after the table-banging Khrushchev era. Less obvious was to be the manner in which Brezhnev would slowly proceed in the years ahead to engross power and establish himself as the new controlling force in Soviet politics.

Brezhnev's Struggle for Ascendancy: 1964-1975

In 1964 Leonid Brezhnev, as party General Secretary, formed only one element of what was a new five-man 'Collective Leadership'. At his side were Mikhail Suslov, Alexander Shelepin, Nikolai Podgorny and Alexei Kosygin. Suslov, at 62, was in 1964 the longest serving member of the Central Committee, Secretariat and Politburo, having joined these bodies in 1941, 1947 and 1955 respectively. He controlled the ideology section of the Secretariat and was anxious to pursue a conservative policy line and maintain party primacy. Shelepin (44), who was a close ally of Suslov, had enjoyed a meteoric rise as head of the Komsomol and KGB and, since 1961, as a party Secretary and chief of the Party-State Control Committee. He had played an important role in ensuring KGB acquiescence to the ousting of Khrushchev and was rewarded in consequence with full membership of the Politburo in November 1964. Podgorny (61), an erstwhile supporter of both Khrushchev and Kozlov, boasted both party and state government experience. He had served as party leader in the Ukraine and had entered the Politburo in May 1960 and the Secretariat in June 1963. By November 1964 he was the

Secretariat's second most influential member, controlling its Organisation Department. Kosygin (60), was an experienced state government administrator with an expertise in economics. He had served as Finance Minister, Chairman of Gosplan and as First Deputy Prime Minister and gained entry to the Politburo in May 1960. Being appointed Prime Minister in October 1964, he formed the second pillar in the 'collective leadership' team of 1964-75.

This new 'collective leadership' had been hastily forced together by feelings of self preservation in October 1964. They were agreed, however, on the fundamentals of style and policy approach that they desired for the future. They were, firstly, determined that no one figure should be allowed to accumulate power and dominate in the personalised manner of Stalin or Khrushchev and that no new 'cult of personality' should be generated. They sought instead to rule in a collegiate, cabinet fashion of bargained compromise, with its principal leaders adopting low public profiles. The new leadership sought, secondly, to continue with the broad outlines of Khrushchev's post-Stalin policy programme, but to implement it in a more guarded manner. They supported Khrushchev's abandonment of rule by terror, his regularisation of the state and party political system and his desire to raise living standards and humanise the CPSU state. They believed, however, that he had gone too far in his attack on élite privileges, in his decentralisation programme, in his party democratisation reforms and in his defence and foreign policy strategy. Cautious change and conservative consolidation were to be the watchwords of the next two decades.

The new leadership moved rapidly to dismantle the more radical and destabilising aspects of the Khrushchev reform programme. It re-established the rayon party committees and ended the experiment with separate agricultural and industrial branches in November 1964 and dismantled the sovnarkhozy regional councils and restored central industrial ministries in September 1965. This satisfied upper party and state bureaucrats who had provided the essential support for the October 1964 'ouster'. Differences existed, however, within the new 'collective leadership' over priorities in the years after 1965. These divisions were in many respects traditional in nature, with Kosygin and Podgorny, as textile and food technology trained leaders of the state bureaucracy, seeking to give a greater priority to raising investment in consumer goods industries at the expense of the defence sector and seeking to combine central planning with the grant of greater autonomy to lower level managers, while Brezhnev and Suslov, whose careers had been primarily spent inside the party machine, gave greater priority to strong party control, the heavy industry-defence sector and to reliance on moral exhortation rather than material incentives.

These ideological differences formed the basis for what became an extended political and personal battle between Brezhnev on the one side and Kosygin and Podgorny on the other for control of the Soviet polity in the years between 1964 and 1970 which shattered the true collectivist spirit of October 1964. It was to be Leonid Brezhnev who was to emerge as the victor from this power struggle, establishing himself by the later 1960s as the dominant force in Soviet politics, ensuring in the process party dominance over the state government machine. His greater patronage resources and his wily political cunning proved decisive in tipping the scales in this contest. The power struggle was, however, conducted in a far more civilised manner than had been evident during the Stalin or Khrushchev eras. There existed a mutual respect for the abilities and experience of each participant and a feeling of a common membership of an exclusive and privileged political élite. Widespread purges were thus avoided. Instead, opponents were gracefully retired or left in office with reduced responsibilities and influence. Secondly, although effective political power progressively gravitated towards Brezhnev during the years between 1964 and 1970, his assumption of authority was never fully complete. He was forced to compromise with important 'institutional interest groups' and he chose to share power with and involve colleagues and rivals in the decision-making process, being anxious not to isolate and expose himself in the manner of the risk-taking Khrushchev.

Brezhnev's political ascendancy in the years between 1964 and 1975 was a slow-moving cumulative process, passing through a series of important stages. Initially, during the period between 1965 and 1968, he was forced to share power clearly with prime minister Kosygin in a party-state duumvirate in which Kosygin took the lead in domestic economic policy-making and played the most active role in overseas diplomacy, while Brezhnev was left to control party affairs, culture and ideology and to make ad hoc interventions in the agricultural sphere. During this period, however, Brezhnev skilfully began to move to isolate and weaken the power bases of his

27

coalition rivals, while at the same time strengthening his own position through the induction into the party and state machines of close allies from his Ukraine, Moldavia, Moscow and Kazakhstan days.

This first became evident in December 1965 when Nikolai Podgorny was removed from the Secretariat and elevated to the State Presidency, while at the same time two former Dnepropetrovsk associates of the party leader, Venyamin Dymshits and Nikolai Tikhonov, were brought into the government machine as Deputy Prime Ministers to work alongside Kosygin. During the next two years four further sets of personnel changes served to strengthen decisively Brezhnev's position within the Soviet polity. He, firstly, gained control over the Secretariat machine by moving in his old Dnieper valley colleague Andrei Kirilenko in April 1966 and ousting his personal rival Alexander Shelepin in June 1967. He, secondly, established a firm hold over the Central Committee apparatus by drafting in the loyal Fyodor Kulakov, Ivan Kapitonov, Konstantin Chernenko, Georgiy Pavlov, Sergei Trapeznikov, Konstantin Rusakov and Vasily Shauro to head key departments. Brezhnev, thirdly, gained the support of the police and security forces through the appointments of Nikolai Shchelokov as Minister of the Interior (September 1966) and Yuri Andropov as KGB chief (May 1967), with Viktor Chebrikov and General Georgy Tsinev as his two deputies. Three of these men, Shchelokov, Chebrikov and Tsinev, had been old Ukraine region allies of the new party leader, while the fourth, Andropov, was a close friend who had worked under Brezhnev during his period at the party Secretariat between 1956-60. Brezhnev finally strengthened his already firm support base among the military during this period with the appointment, in March 1967, of Marshal Andrei Grechko, an old wartime colleague in arms, as the country's new Defence Minister.

The growing political influence of Leonid Brezhnev during the years between 1967 and 1970 was reflected in an increased conservatism in the Soviet Union's foreign and domestic policy stance. At home, following Kosygin's brief but abortive attempts at reform between 1964-66, a tougher economic and ideological line was adopted, with the emphasis being placed on discipline, moral exhortation and party control in the economic sphere rather than on material incentives. Defence spending was also given a new and higher priority, while, overseas, Soviet troops were employed to crush Alexander Dubcek's liberalisation experiment in Czechoslovakia in August 1968 in an early example of what later became termed the 'Brezhnev doctrine'.

Between 1970 and 1973 Brezhnev's political authority was further extended and his public profile as party leader began to be advanced in a presidential manner. Brezhnev now took over control of economic policy-making, having the major say in the framing of the new 1971-75 Five Year Plan, and foreign affairs, while his tours and speeches were given prominent media coverage in what formed part of a slow and tentative development of a Brezhnevite 'cult of personality'. This growing dominance of the Soviet political scene was underlined and buttressed by events at the 24th CPSU Congress in March 1971 during which the party leader delivered a marathon six-hour address which was broadcast live across the nation. At the same conference Brezhnev gained majority control over the new Central Committee and secured the election of four allies, Vladimir Shcherbitsky (Ukraine Party Leader), Dinmukhamed Kunayev (Kazakhstan Party Leader), Fyodor Kulakov (Agriculture Secretary) and Viktor Grishin (Moscow Party Chief) on to the new, and enlarged, Politburo.

The 1971 CPSU Congress established Leonid Brezhnev as the controlling force in Soviet politics. It was followed by a number of novel policy initiatives which also displayed the flexibility and pragmatism of the party leader. At home, for example, inspirited by the outbreak of food riots in Gdansk in Poland, a greater emphasis was given to raising the production of consumer goods. Overseas a new, and more moderate, policy of 'détente' with the West was put into effect, with the party leader travelling to Bonn and Washington in 1973 to negotiate new peace accords.

However, despite the vigour of Leonid Brezhnev during these years, his authority was by no means absolute and remained subject to checks and limits. For example, he attempted in 1970-71 to oust Kosygin from his post as Prime Minister so as to combine leadership of both the party and state machines in a Khrushchevian manner. Brezhnev failed, however, to gain the support of his wary colleagues for this move and was forced to continue to concede significant elements of authority to Kosygin and the state machine. Brezhnev, secondly, remained anxious to share out decision-making responsibility among élite groups in a risk-reducing manner and to delay action until unanimous agreement had been achieved. Such a leadership approach suited Brezhnev's cautious, consensual 'political broker' personality and survivalist instinct. It became fully institutionalised in April 1973 when three of the key and previously excluded Soviet interest group leaders — Marshal Grechko (Minister of Defence), Andrei Gromyko (Foreign

Politics in the Soviet Union

Minister) and Yuri Andropov (KGB Chief) — were inducted into the Politburo to participate directly in the policy-making process. Such an approach proved to be of considerable political value in securing Brezhnev's leadership position, but had adverse consequences for the Soviet economy and society, encouraging the postponement of decision taking on difficult and controversial issues and the search instead for easy, painless, fudged solutions.

Brezhnev's Slow Decline: 1975-1982

In January 1975 Leonid Brezhnev presided over a bloated Politburo of 16 full and 8 'candidate' members, with an average age of 64 and 60 years respectively, and a 10-man Secretariat. (See Table 1.) The former body had been allowed to steadily grow in size in the years since 1964 as a result of the General Secretary's predisposition for appointing new members to improve his own position rather than purging existing members. Through such a process Brezhnev could rely on strong support from a core of Politburo members — Kunayev, Kulakov, Shcherbitsky, Kirilenko and Grechko — and ad hoc support on varying issues from different other members, for example Andropov, Grishin, Suslov, Pelshe, Gromyko and Mazurov, to provide secure majorities on most of the party leader's policy initiatives. In the years between 1975 and 1977 Brezhnev's majority within the Politburo was further strengthened by the deposition of two opponents, Alexander Shelepin (April 1975) and Dmitri Polyanski (February 1976), and their replacement by Grigori Romanov and Dmitri Ustinov: the latter also became Minister of Defence following Marshal Grechko's death in April 1976.

With this strengthened power base, Leonid Brezhnev reached the apogee of his political career in 1976 and 1977. He dominated the 25th Party Congress in February 1976, each speech delivered containing a line of personal praise for Brezhnev. He was granted the title of 'Marshal of the Soviet Union' and 'Commander-in-Chief' of the Soviet armed forces and oversaw the construction of a new state constitution in 1977. In this constitution the new post of vice chairman to the Praesidium of the Supreme Soviet was created to which routine ceremonial tasks were assigned. This enabled Brezhnev to finally remove Podgorny as President (ousting him at the same time from the Politburo) in May 1977 and combine the posts of head of state and Party General Secretary, thus establishing the *de jure* as well as *de facto* supremacy of the party leader in the

30

TABLE 1 : THE CPSU POLITBURO AND SECRETARIAT IN JANUARY 1975

POLITBURO

Full Members	Age		First Elected	Removed or Died
LI Brezhnev	(68)	General Secretary	1957	d. 1982
DA Kunayev	(62)	Kazakhstan Pty Ldr	1971	r. 1987
YV Andropov	(61)	Chief of KGB	1971	d. 1984
KT Mazurov	(60)	lst Deputy PM	1965	r. 1978
AA Grechko	(71)	Defence Minister	1973	d. 1976
AY Pelshe	(75)	Chmn Pty Control Cmm	1966	r. 1982
VV Grishin	(60)	Moscow Pty Ldr	1971	r. 1985
NV Podgorny	(71)	State President	1960	r. 1977
AA Gromyko	(66)	Foreign Minister	1973	
DC Polyanski	(60)	Agriculture Minister	1960	r. 1976
AP Kirilenko	(67)	Secretariat	1962	r. 1982
VV Shcherbitsky	(57)	Ukraine Pty Ldr	1971	
AN Kosygin	(70)	Prime Minister	1960	d. 1980
AN Shelepin	(56)	Trade Union Chief	1964	r. 1975
FD Kulakov	(57)	Secretariat	1971	d. 1978
MA Suslov	(72)	Secretariat	1955	d. 1982

CANDIDATES

PN Demichev	(56)	Secretariat
PM Masherov	(57)	Byelorussia Pty Ldr
SR Rashidov	(57)	Uzbekistan Pty Ldr
GV Romanov	(52)	Leningrad Pty Ldr
MS Solomentsev	(61)	Russian Fed. PM
DF Ustinov	(67)	Secretariat
GA Aliyev	(52)	Azerbaijan Pty Ldr
BN Ponomarev	(68)	Secretariat

SECRETARIAT

LI Brezhnev	(68)	General Secretary
PN Demichev	(56)	Culture
VI Dolgikh	(51)	Heavy Industry
IV Kapitonov	(59)	Cadres Dept.
KF Katushev	(47)	Overseas CP Relations
AP Kirilenko	(67)	Organisation
FD Kulakov	(57)	Agriculture
BN Ponomarev	(68)	Foreign Affairs
MA Suslov	(72)	Ideology
DF Ustinov	(67)	Defence

Soviet system of government. Brezhnev further extended his influence over the state sphere of government by appointing his old, loyal Dnepropetrovsk colleague Nikolai Tikhonov as First Deputy Prime Minister in October 1976. Tikhonov, who entered the Politburo in 1979, proceeded to take over progressively the administrative reins of the state government as Alexei Kosygin's health began to deteriorate and he became Prime Minister in his own right following Kosygin's death in December 1980.

Brezhnev's period of personal dominance proved, however, to be short-lived. Ailing personal health began to weaken the grip of a man who had been renowned during the 1960s and early 1970s, particularly overseas, for his drive, energy and boisterousness. In 1975 and 1977 Brezhnev suffered two serious strokes and was forced to have a pacemaker fitted and undergo facial surgery. This visibly sapped the strength and energies of the party leader in the final quinquennium of his life. His speech became slurred, his movement shaky and he began to vanish for months on end to rest at treatment clinics in the Crimea. This forced Brezhnev to delegate policy-making increasingly to his personal aides and the private office machine, led by Konstantin Chernenko, as well as to share power with other Politburo members in a renewed collectivist fashion.

The final years of the Brezhnev administration thus became ones of policy sclerosis and general drift. With regard to policy-making, they were ones of growing conservatism at home, under the influence of the centralising First Deputy Prime Minister Nikolai Tikhonov and the KGB Chief Yuri Andropov, as well as abroad, where détente began to give way to a renewed 'cold war', particularly following the Soviet invasion of Afghanistan in December 1979. Above all, however, the period was dominated by the deaths of leading figures from the Brezhnevite old guard — Fyodor Kulakov (July 1978), Alexei Kosygin (December 1980), Mikhail Suslov (January 1982) — with the consequent shrinking in size of the Politburo and the emergence of a mounting succession struggle for the Brezhnev crown.

Brezhnev himself had been careful throughout his lengthy career not to establish an obvious second-in-command successor in case he found himself being challenged and ousted. In his final years, however, he abandoned this strategy and began to single out one close aide, Konstantin Chernenko, for special promotion.

Konstantin Chernenko was born in September 1911 into a 'Great Russian' peasant farming family which had settled in the village of

Bolshaya Tes in Central Siberia. He joined the Komsomol in 1929 and the Communist Party in 1931 and was educated at the party's organisation school. He first worked for his native Krasnoyarsk Territorial (*kray*) Party Committee between 1933-43, emerging as a specialist in political propaganda, and then, following further training at the Higher Party School in Moscow, was appointed secretary of the Penza district (rayon) committee within Central Russia, before moving to Moldavia as head of the propaganda department in 1948. Here, he came into contact with, and impressed, Leonid Brezhnev, who adopted Chernenko as his ADC and brought him to Moscow to work in the central apparatus in 1956. In 1965, with Brezhnev installed as party General Secretary, Chernenko was appointed head of the Central Committee's powerful General Department, an administrative department through which all top-secret messages to Politburo members are channelled. In 1971 he was elected a member of the CPSU Central Committee and subsequently proceeded to gain rapid promotion into, first, the Secretariat (March 1976) and then the Politburo (as a 'candidate' in October 1977 and as a full member in December 1978) during the later Brezhnev years. Chernenko also began increasingly to accompany Brezhnev on his overseas visits, was given third ranking standing on official occasions and was allowed to chair Politburo and Secretariat meetings in the party leader's absence.

However, while Brezhnev himself was seeking to promote his protégé Chernenko, another figure within the Politburo, the KGB chief Yuri Andropov began to emerge as a rival candidate for the succession in the years between 1978 and 1982 and began to gain increasing political influence. This was reflected by heightened KGB campaigns against internal intellectual and religious dissidence and by the election of the Georgian Party chief and ex-Georgian KGB chief, Edward Shevardnadze, as a Politburo candidate member and by the induction of the 47-year-old Stavropol region boss, Mikhail Gorbachev, into the Secretariat as Agriculture Secretary in December 1978, both emerging as close allies of the KGB chief. (Gorbachev was subsequently promoted to 'candidate' status in the Politburo in 1979 and to full membership in October 1980). In January 1982, following the death of Mikhail Suslov, Andropov resigned his KGB post and entered the Secretariat itself as the new ideology supremo and thus its second ranking figure.

Ten months later Leonid Brezhnev, on 10 November 1982,

suffered a final, fatal stroke and died at the age of 75. This brought the succession struggle to a head. Whoever took over would face a difficult task, needing to address the problems and rigidities which had been allowed to develop in the Soviet polity and economy during the Brezhnev era.

The Brezhnev Era: An Assessment

The Brezhnev era had been one of caution and conservatism in which there was a constant search to compromise with and 'buy off' potential institutional opponents rather than take radical, risk-taking initiatives. This had some advantages at home, where a new stability was given to the state-party political system in which the limits of tolerance and dissent were made clear. The new 1977 constitution, with its theme of harmonious 'developed socialism', was the distilled essence of this 'Brezhnev system'. In addition, the Brezhnev era also saw regular and significant supra 3% per annum per capita increases in consumption standards, a marked levelling in income differentials and the launch of major housebuilding, education and health programmes, as a genuine effort was made to eradicate poverty and establish a new socialist 'welfare state'. Finally, abroad (see Part 3), the Brezhnev era saw the Soviet Union at last establish itself as a global superpower, attaining strategic military parity with the United States and gaining *de facto* Western recognition of its control over its post-war East European 'empire' at the 1975 Helsinki conference.

The conservative and consensual Brezhnev approach to political affairs had, however, significant costs for Soviet society and for the economy. Firstly, it entailed the continuation of centralised political and ideological control, although of a more limited and humane nature than that experienced during the Stalin era, and the maintenance of an unusually high level of defence spending. Secondly, during the Brezhnev years there were only tinkering attempts to inject new efficiency into the Soviet economy and a shying away from radical market-orientated or decentralist reform programmes. In consequence, the Soviet economic growth rate became sluggish and per capita living standards fell progressively behind the West. Thirdly, the party leader's concern to maintain harmonious relations with the apparatchiki élite led him to introduce a system of 'stability of cadres' in contradistinction to Khrushchev's policy of cadre rotation. The result of such a policy was a stultifying of the state and party bureaucracies, and a growth in corruption at middle and upper bureaucrat levels.[1] Brezhnev, who himself enjoyed in private the élite perks of fast cars, dacha retreats, expensive food and drink and foreign luxuries, turned a blind eye to such apparatchiki misdemeanours. The consequence was, however, the development of public contempt for party leaders, whose moralising in the economic sphere for discipline, self sacrifice and Stakhavonite 'socialist emulation' fell increasingly on deaf ears.

The Andropov Administration: 1982-1984

Andropov's Accession to Power

With Mikhail Suslov dead and Andrei Kirilenko and Arvid Pelshe incapacitated by failing health, the battle between Yuri Andropov and Konstantin Chernenko to succeed Leonid Brezhnev intensified during the summer and autumn months of 1982. It proved, however, to be the former KGB man, Yuri Andropov, who emerged victorious from this power struggle, building up a powerful coalition of 'institutional interest group' leaders behind his candidature.

Andropov proposed a new reformist programme to stimulate the sluggish Soviet economy without risking ideological or political integrity. It involved a strict anti-corruption campaign and a number of minor economic innovations which were aimed at raising production efficiency. The Andropov programme sought, in addition, by strengthening the Soviet economic base, to improve its military defence capability, thus enabling the nation to continue to play a dominant role on the world stage and to compete with a rapidly rearming United States. Such a policy approach offered a mixture of continuity and change which appealed in particular to the Soviet military élite, who abhorred bureaucratic corruption and who were anxious to foster industrial modernisation for defence reasons. In 1982 this defence lobby, which was led by Marshal Dmitri Ustinov and by the heavy industry supremo Grigori

---

[1] A striking example of such 'stability of cadres' was the fact that, of the 319 full Central Committee members elected by the 26th CPSU Congress in February 1981, 95 had already been full or candidate members as early as 1961 and a further 55 had become members by 1966.

Romanov, formed an unusually powerful and influential grouping within the Politburo. They were joined in their support for Yuri Andropov by the Foreign Minister Andrei Gromyko and the Caucasus agronomist Mikhail Gorbachev in a new 'coalition for change' which combined generals, technocrats and ambitious young party men.

Yuri Andropov's rival for the succession, Konstantin Chernenko, offered, in contrast, a policy of 'stability of the cadres', which appealed to the older and well entrenched regional party élite. This provided Chernenko with a potentially broad base of support in the apparatchiki-dominated CPSU. Chernenko failed, however, in his bid for the leadership in November 1982 for largely personal reasons. Having been a servant rather than leader or administrator in his own right during his lengthy political career, Chernenko lacked an independent power base of his own. He lacked, secondly, a broad and varied political experience, being viewed as an ineffectual, upstart placeman of the former General Secretary; consequently, his new leadership pretensions were resented by the old guard Brezhnevite figures of Kunayev and Shcherbitsky. The third, possibly decisive, reason for Chernenko's failure to wrest the party leadership in November 1982 were his policy statements of 1981-82, in which, speaking against the concept of a 'winnable nuclear war' and promising in the future to give greater priority to agriculture and consumer industries *vis-à-vis* the heavy industry-defence sector, Chernenko decisively alienated the military lobby.

When Brezhnev died during the early hours of 10 November 1982, Chernenko could rely on only the firm support of Prime Minister Tikhonov and the reluctant support of Kunayev. The Andropov faction, aware of Chernenko's isolation, moved rapidly and decisively and called an enlarged Politburo meeting (comprising full and 'candidate' members, Marshals and key Central Committee members) under the chairmanship of Vladimir Shcherbitsky during the afternoon of 10 November. At this meeting Yuri Andropov was proposed for the party General Secretaryship by Marshal Ustinov, it being suggested at the same time that Chernenko might subsequently be made State President. This proposition was carried 'unanimously' and a Central Committee plenum was hastily convened to formally ratify the decision.

The full 319-member Central Committee met on 12 November 1982 and, being dominated by regional apparatchiki bosses who were already suffering from the KGB's continuing anti-corruption campaign, might have been expected to be less than enthusiastic for the Andropov candidature. The anti-Andropov forces, however, were left with insufficient time to organise a counter-coup and were forced to vote in Andropov's favour, following his nomination by Konstantin Chernenko: Chernenko stressing at the same time the need for the new leader to govern in a collectivist and comradely fashion. Thus on 12 November 1982, after 48 hours of secret lobbying, Yuri Andropov was 'unanimously' elected to the leadership of the Communist Party. The transfer of power after 18 years of Brezhnevite rule had been orderly and pacific. This marked a contrast with the more brutal leadership struggles of the years between 1924-27 and 1953-57. In addition, in contrast to 1957 and 1964, the CPSU Central Committee had on this occasion played no overtly decisive role in the succession contest.

Andropov in Power: The Beginning of a New Era?

The new man in control was a 68-year-old, ex-secret policeman with a known heart and liver complaint, who had been assiduously cultivating an image as a tough, but intelligent and reformist, politician anxious to grapple with Russia's economic and administrative inefficiencies. Andropov was not, however, a narrowly specialised policeman or intelligence officer; he had lengthy administrative, party and diplomatic experience.[1]

Born in the village of Nagutskaya in Stavropol province of the North Caucasus region of Southern Russia in June 1914, the son of a middle-class railway official, Andropov trained as a water transport engineer and began work in the shipyards of the upper Volga at Rybinsk in 1930. Here he became an organiser for the local Komsomol and received further education before being appointed head of the Komsomol in the Karelo-Finnish republic in Northern Russia in 1940,[2] following a purge of the local leadership cadres. He was given the task of 'Sovietising' the newly ceded Karelian peninsula but within a year, following the German takeover of the republic, found himself involved instead in organising an

[1] Of Andropov's 46 years in political life before 1982, 27 had been spent as a party functionary, including five years in the Secretariat.

[2] The Karelian peninsula formed a constituent (twelfth) Union Republic of the USSR between 1940-56, before it was downgraded to the rank of an Autonomous Republic within the RSFSR.

anti-German partisan resistance movement. After the war, Andropov was promoted to the post of second party secretary in Karelia and proved so successful that he was brought to Moscow in 1951 to work for the CPSU Central Committee. After two years with this body, Andropov was sent to the Soviet embassy in Hungary and became ambassador in Budapest between 1954-57, and had the task of arresting leading dissident politicians when Soviet tanks crushed the Hungarian uprising in 1956. It was in this post that he first impressed and caught the eye of the strict party ideologue Mikhail Suslov, who was to become Andropov's patron. Andropov subsequently returned to the Central Committee as head of the department dealing with foreign communist parties in 1957 and was inducted into the Secretariat in 1962. Five years later he was appointed KGB chief by General Secretary Brezhnev, becoming a full member of the Politburo in 1973. As head of the KGB, Andropov gained a reputation for the tough and economical use of secret police terror in crushing the dissident movement and fighting corruption. This reputation worried political observers in the West as Andropov acceded to the Soviet leadership during a period of acute tension in East-West relations. It was, however, the economic reforms of Andropov, and the promise of greater changes to come, which were to be the distinguishing feature of his brief administration.

These economic reforms will be dealt with in Part 4. In this section attention is focused instead upon political changes. The first and most noticeable of these developments was the speed with which Yuri Andropov was able to take over diverse levers of power and exert firm and distinctive control. He did not fully remove his rival Konstantin Chernenko, who gained and held on to the important post of party Secretary in charge of ideology, but he was able to shift the Soviet machine in his chosen direction.

By November 1982 the recent deaths and retirements of elder Politburo members had reduced the size of this body to only ten members. Andropov was thus in a position to promote younger supporters and likeminded men to help strengthen his position. Within a fortnight of his accession he had promoted the 59-year-old Geidar Aliyev from 'candidate' to full Politburo membership combined with the post of First Deputy Prime Minister).[1] Aliyev, an austere KGB man, had been a successful party leader in Azerbaijan

[1] Aliyev was an Azeri Muslim by birth who had made his reputation purging the corrupt former Azerbaijani party leadership in the late 1960s.

since 1969, being involved more recently with anti-corruption drives. The 69-year-old Russian republic premier Mikhail Solomentsev was also promoted to replace the late Arvid Pelshe as chairman of the Party Control Commission in June 1983. Grigori Romanov, the 60-year-old Leningrad party chief, was also moved during this reshuffle (see Table 2) into the Party Secretariat — concentrating on heavy industries, utilising his Leningrad experience, while Mikhail Gorbachev looked after agriculture and the broader economy. Yegor Ligachev (a former Siberian district chief) was placed in the Central Committee in charge of party appointments, to give Andropov a firmer grip over the party apparatus. The 57-year-old district party chief Vitaly Vorotnikov and Mikhail Solomentsev were two final additions to the Politburo team in December 1983, with the KGB's new chief, Viktor Chebrikov, joining as a 'candidate'.[2] In the Central Committee, Andropov appointed new chiefs to 9 of the 23 departments, including Nikolai Ryzhkov (b. 1929), the young former head of the giant Uralmash engineering combine and first deputy chairman of Gosplan, who became head of an expanded economics department concerned with co-ordinating domestic industry and foreign trade. Such additions brought in more imaginative and technocratic policy makers with a new and more dynamic no-nonsense approach.

These changes and the assumption of the Supreme Soviet Presidency in June 1983 (breaking an earlier promise made to Chernenko), only seven months after his accession to the party leadership, outwardly suggested that Yuri Andropov had quickly gathered in the reins of power and had established a dominant position which it had taken Brezhnev a decade to achieve. However, there is evidence that the conservative lobby centred around Chernenko — a grouping which included middle-ranking party apparatchiks concerned with their privileges and sinecures and with the plans to curb their rights to interfere in the management of factories and farms — were still a force to be reckoned with and blocked the appointment of even more Andropov supporters to the Politburo. This group gained some support from a number of military men who had become worried about the political consequences of over-rapid reform.

---

[1] Chebrikov had become KGB chief in December 1982 when his predecessor, Vitaly Fedorchuk, was moved to take over the Ministry of Internal Affairs (in charge of internal uniformed police) from the lax Brezhnevite Nikolai Shchelokov.

TABLE 2 : THE CPSU POLITBURO AND SECRETARIAT IN JULY 1983

POLITBURO

Full Members	Age	
YV Andropov	(69)	General Secretary
GA Aliyev	(60)	1st Deputy PM
KU Chernenko	(71)	Secretariat
MS Gorbachev	(52)	Secretariat
VV Grishin	(68)	Moscow Pty Ldr
AA Gromyko	(74)	Foreign Minister
DA Kunayev	(70)	Kazakhstan Pty Ldr
GV Romanov	(60)	Secretariat
VV Shcherbitsky	(65)	Ukraine Pty Ldr
NA Tikhonov	(78)	Prime Minister
DF Ustinov	(74)	Defence Minister

CANDIDATES

PM Demichev	(64)	Minister of Culture
VI Dolgikh	(59)	Secretariat
TY Kiselev	(65)	Byelorussia Pty Ldr
VV Kuznetsov	(81)	Dpty (Acting) President
BN Ponomarev	(77)	Secretariat
SR Rashidov	(65)	Uzbekistan Pty Ldr
EA Shevardnadze	(54)	Georgian Pty Ldr
MS Solomentsev	(69)	Party Control Cmm

SECRETARIAT

YV Andropov	(69)	General Secretary
KU Chernenko	(71)	General/Ideology
VI Dolgikh	(59)	Industry
MS Gorbachev	(52)	Agriculture
IV Kapitonov	(67)	Organisation
BN Ponomarev	(77)	Foreign Affairs
GV Romanov	(60)	Heavy Industry
KV Rusakov	(73)	Overseas CP Liaison
NI Ryzhkov	(53)	The Economy
MV Zimyanin	(69)	Propaganda/Culture

Andropov, recognising the obstacles to economic change, decided to shake up the stagnant oblast (regional) level of the party machine. Under Brezhnev oblast regional party secretaryships had become jobs awarded for life. They formed significant intermediate fiefships in charge of areas several times the size of Britain and with populations of many millions — carrying out, delaying or ignoring orders handed down from Moscow. Andropov saw these office holders as key obstructions who were holding back his economic reforms, and as potential allies to the do-nothing Chernenko, and, since oblast chiefs made up a third of the CPSU Central Committee, as obstacles in the way of the promotion of more of his supporters into the party hierarchy. He thus organised a press campaign in September 1983 — calling for a closer look at the records of party officials, the replacement of those who were not doing their job properly and the reshuffling of a number of lower posts — which recalled Khrushchev's abortive Rule 25 campaign in 1961. Then in December 1983 and January 1984 elections were held, supervised by Gorbachev and Ligachev, for the more than 150 oblast chief posts, with the aim of replacing more than a third of the total, to give Andropov a firmer hold over the Central Committee. This shake-up was in the end, however, only partly successful. By February 1984, 34, or around a fifth, of oblast chiefs had been replaced, but less than half of these had been a result of the elections. The deterioration in Andropov's personal health from August 1983 had persuaded regional party officials against challenging their local chiefs in the name of a man whose future was uncertain. In the big industrial centres, in particular, Brezhnev men held on to their seats and were in a position to block economic reforms.

Yuri Andropov's campaign to make the party more effective and responsive had thus only been partially implemented when its architect finally succumbed to a combination of heart and kidney disease on 9 February 1984 after less than 15 months in office. He had been busily grooming a group of technocratic successors — Gorbachev, Aliyev, Ligachev, Ryzhkov — who were soon to continue his reforms. However, it was his older rival Konstantin Chernenko who was to be the temporary stop-gap replacement in a Politburo still not fully wedded to the necessity of reform.

The Chernenko Interregnum: 1984-1985

The choice of Konstantin Chernenko, the man passed over only 15 months previously, as the new CPSU General Secretary on 13 February 1984 was a choice of caution and uncertainty. Chernenko, once tagged as the man who had carried Brezhnev's bags and opened his mail, was a party servant with no clear policies or abilities. His appointment served, however, the purposes of party apparatchiks who were concerned with the

Andropov corruption drives, reshuffles and oblast elections, as well as military chiefs who were opposed to radical changes. His election marked in many respects a return to the later Brezhnev conservative era.

In contrast to Yuri Andropov, Konstantin Chernenko surrounded himself with the older guard of Gromyko, Ustinov, Grishin and Tikhonov, who had reluctantly supported his election. Under this new administration the party corruption campaigns were dropped and perks once again tolerated and a small 'cult of personality' was unsuccessfully developed. Within two months Konstantin Chernenko had swiftly gathered together the triumvirate of key posts — General Secretary, Commander-in-Chief and President — which it had taken Yuri Andropov seven months to acquire. Chernenko's authority was, however, greatly inhibited not only by heart and lung disease (which was clearly visible, forcing prolonged absences, after July 1984), but also by the continuing strength of his rivals. In particular, the reformist Andropov faction retained significant power, with Mikhail Gorbachev gaining a committee chairmanship (overseeing ideology and personnel) and being recognised as the number two man with a possible veto over important decisions. The debility and inertia of the Chernenko administration was highlighted by the fact that despite the gaps that had been left in a shrunken Politburo of eleven, no new additions were made during this period. The Chernenko era can thus be seen as one of 'collectivist' control, with Gorbachev retaining a significant say over economic affairs and Gromyko and Ustinov over foreign affairs.

One significant development during the Chernenko era centred, however, around changes in the military hierarchy, with the roots for these changes revolving around the conflict between the military's demand for increased resources (as the arms race gained pace and as equipment became more sophisticated) and the demands of the domestic economy.

The extrovert and bullish chief-of-staff, Marshal Nikolai Ogarkov, had long argued for the need for the Soviet Union to keep up with the West in the development of sophisticated conventional weapons and to develop high-technology defensive control systems akin to the US 'Star Wars' programme. However, such a programme was a resource threat both to the traditional 'lower-technology' heavy defence industries run by Ustinov and Romanov, and to the civilian economy directed by

Gorbachev. Ogarkov, who was blamed for overselling the SS-20 missile programme in the later 1970s, thus provoking Western counter-deployments, and for the 1983 shooting down of a South Korean passenger jet, was now ousted and replaced by the more pliable Marshal Sergei Akhromeev (a member of the party's Central Committee since 1983). Within four months there was a further, this time natural, departure from the military establishment with the death of Dmitri Ustinov in December 1984. Ustinov had worked his way up through the defence industries as a civilian, but he was to be replaced as Defence Minister by a 73-year-old professional soldier, Marshal Sergei Sokolov, who had recently been overseeing the Afghanistan campaign. This appointment of a military man as Defence Minister represented a return to tradition. But the exclusion of Sokolov from the Politburo weakened the direct influence of the military in the highest organs of power and suggested a diminution in military *vis-à-vis* party influence over policy decisions.

Gorbachev — The Reformer: 1985 –

A Smooth Transfer of Power: The 1985 Succession Struggle

Konstantin Chernenko's reign as party leader was the briefest and least consequential in Soviet history. After an initial hectic four months of factory visits, handshaking and ceremonial presentations, Russia's emphysemic leader disappeared to a Crimean health retreat in July 1984, to be glimpsed only briefly in December, before finally dying on 10 March 1985 after barely a year in the highest office. Chernenko's short administration had served only to put a temporary brake on a number of the administrative and economic reforms actuated by Yuri Andropov, and to give additional time for the ambitious younger generation of Politburo members to gain the necessary support, stature and authority which they had lacked in February 1984.

Mikhail Gorbachev (the protégé of Mikhail Suslov and Yuri Andropov), in particular, used this year to press his claims for the General Secretaryship. By March 1985 he was confronted with only one rival who combined the two key positions of a Central Committee Secretaryship and a position in the Politburo — the 61-year-old Grigori Romanov. Romanov, at the age of 47 had been made party boss in Leningrad, giving him control of the second largest party machine in the country. He reorganised the city's heavy industry and effected significant advances in housing, working conditions and managerial efficiency. This gained him a seat on the Politburo in 1976, but his career had then stagnated before Yuri Andropov promoted him to the Party Secretariat in June 1983. Romanov brought with him a reputation as an ideological hardliner opposed to any form of political relaxation, and as a sabre-rattling xenophobe. His prescription for Russia's economic ills was stricter discipline and tighter management and direction. This programme appealed to the military hierarchy, but in the end a combination of factors blocked Romanov's election as General Secretary. Firstly, he lacked the necessary Moscow connections and power base; secondly, the military were voiceless in the Politburo in 1985; and thirdly, he unfortunately shared the former Tsarist royal family name and had gained a reputation for extravagance, intemperance and arrogance. The most damaging story in circulation suggested that he had purloined a Catherine the Great dinner service from the Hermitage museum for his daughter's boisterous wedding party — only later returning it minus a number of priceless pieces. Romanov's personality undoubtedly rekindled memories of Josef Stalin and was an important factor in dissuading anxious Politburo colleagues from casting a vote in his favour.

In the absence of sufficient support for Grigori Romanov the only alternative to Gorbachev lay in the elder Brezhnevist septuagenarian generation. Chernenko's brief tenure had, however, been sufficient to remove (through death) the chief such contender, Dmitri Ustinov. Two other candidates, the republican party bosses Kunayev and Shcherbitsky lacked a Moscow base and were not of full 'Great Russian' stock. Only the safe, but mediocre, Viktor Grishin (70), the Moscow party boss who had been a full Politburo member since 1971 and possessed also considerable trade union experience, was left to carry the standard of the old guard.

The balance of forces in the Politburo and Central Committee had, however, been slowly changing since 1978 and particularly since the onset of the Andropov administration, with the slow atrophy of the Brezhnev generation and the upward movement of a somewhat more reformist generation. Thus, the ten-man Politburo in March 1985 could be seen as almost evenly divided between the 'old guard' and the economic reformers, but with only seven members present in Moscow on 10 March, the balance was tilted towards the latter group. Chernenko sent a message from his deathbed giving his support to Viktor Grishin, whose name was formally proposed by Grigori Romanov. But Mikhail Gorbachev, at 54, three years younger than Leonid Brezhnev when he assumed the General Secretaryship in 1964, proved to be the most obvious and acceptable choice as party leader. Proposed by Andrei Gromyko and seconded by KGB chief Viktor Chebrikov, on 11 March 1986, Gorbachev became party leader in one of the smoothest transfers of power in Soviet history.

The Making of a General Secretary: Gorbachev's pre-1985 Background

Mikhail Sergeevich Gorbachev had enjoyed a charmed and, by Soviet standards, a meteoric career, in which he had been marked out for high office from an early age. He came from a humble background, being the son of a 'Great Russian' agricultural mechanic born in Privolnoye village in the North Caucasus region of Southern Russia on 2 March 1931. Gorbachev, however, distinguished himself at school, gaining the 'Red Banner of Labour Group' decoration, and, benefiting from the expansion of educational opportunity during the later 1940s, was sent by his municipality to the prestigious Moscow University in 1950. Here Gorbachev mixed with leading contemporaries and took a degree in law which opened his mind up to novel and cosmopolitan ideas. He also met and married a bright, young philosophy student Raisa (b. 1933), before returning to his home region of Stavropol (North Caucasus) to begin work for the CPSU, which he had joined in 1952.

For seven years after 1955 Gorbachev worked for the Komsomol in Stavropol. In 1962, however, he switched over to the party machine, being chosen by the regional chief Fyodor Kulakov (1960-64) to oversee agriculture. Gorbachev displayed considerable enthusiasm for this new post, taking an external degree in agronomy at the Stavropol Institute of Agriculture while his wife Raisa wrote a pioneering PhD on rural social conditions in Stavropol. During the next eight years he moved up the party ladder within the Stavropol region, finally becoming party First Secretary in April 1970. He had thus, by the age of 39, entered the uppermost ranks of the CPSU apparatus. In 1970 Gorbachev also became a member of the Supreme Soviet and a year later was inducted into the CPSU's influential Central Committee.

As Regional Secretary in Stavropol, Gorbachev developed a reputation as an honest and industrious managerial technocrat who sharply contrasted with the corrupt and complacent Brezhnevite agit-prop politicians who were in control of the majority of Soviet republics and regions during these years. He was an avid 'improver' who was constantly searching for ways to raise output and living standards during the early 1970s. He also took a great personal interest in local affairs. Pushing managers and local officials hard, he emerged as a strict disciplinarian and displayed a flair for leadership.

Despite these obvious abilities, however, Gorbachev's promotion further up the CPSU party machine resulted in a large degree from the influential connections that he was able to make in the Stavropol region. Three figures, Mikhail Suslov, Fyodor Kulakov and Yuri Andropov, emerged as crucial patrons. Mikhail Suslov, the second most powerful figure within the the CPSU during the 1970s, had served as Stavropol Region First Secretary between 1939 and 1944 and maintained close links with his old fief, regularly holidaying in his summer dacha retreat near the Black Sea. This austere and imposing figure, while far more hardline and conservative in his outlook than Gorbachev, was impressed by Gorbachev's record as an administrator and helped to promote his career during the early 1970s. Fyodor Kulakov, Gorbachev's earliest patron who was by the 1970s a Politburo member and CPSU Secretary for Agriculture, provided vital secondary support. It was, however, the emerging figure of Yuri Andropov who was to prove to be Gorbachev's most important ally in Moscow. Andropov, who was born within the Stavropol region and who regularly came to Kislovodsk mineral spa for treatment for his liver and kidney complaints[1], came into close contact with his countryman Gorbachev and found reflected in him many of his own views and values. His support proved vital in Gorbachev's induction into the CPSU Secretariat as Agriculture

[1] Other prominent CPSU leaders, including Kosygin, visited the Stavropol health spas, while Brezhnev enjoyed a dacha retreat in the neighbouring Krasnodar region.

Secretary in December 1978, following Fyodor Kulakov's death, and into the Politburo in 1979-80.

As Agriculture Secretary, Gorbachev attempted to introduce a number of reforms, but his actual record proved to be disappointing (see Part 4). Indeed, the harvest in 1981 was so disastrous that, but for Brezhnev's incapacity and Andropov's 'protection', Gorbachev might have been sacked and his career ended. Once his patron Andropov gained power in November 1982, however, Gorbachev was able to firmly establish himself as the leading contender for the succession among the new generation of apparatchiks. He was placed in charge of overseeing the economy and party personnel under Andropov and during the Chernenko administration he took over control of party ideology and became the party's unofficial deputy leader in what was a 'dual key' administration. Gorbachev also gained foreign policy experience during these years, visiting Canada as Agriculture Secretary in May 1983 and in June 1984, after assuming the chairmanship of the Foreign Affairs Commission of the Supreme Soviet, he visited Italy for the funeral of the Italian Communist Party chairman Enrico Berlinguer. In December that year he visited Britain and met Margaret Thatcher. Following Konstantin Chernenko's stroke on 27 December 1984, Gorbachev gained effective day-to-day control of the Soviet Union, and three months later he assumed formal leadership of the CPSU.

Gorbachev's Ideas and Policy Aims

The brief sketch above of Gorbachev's background shows him to be a man of intellect, integrity and probity: a committed, puritanical, but flexible leader in the mould of his patron Yuri Andropov. He is also, most importantly, a representative of the new 'third generation' of CPSU leaders. Gorbachev was born after the 1917 Revolution, brought up fully under the communist system, avoided the Stalinist era and the debates over collectivisation and centralisation and was too young to fight in the 'Great Patriotic War'. He thus lacks the prejudices and timidity of many of the older guard Brezhnevites, is better educated and is more technocratic and managerial in outlook.

Gorbachev, whose early party career had been spent during the 1950s and 1960s era of rapid growth, was concerned above all, on assuming power in March 1985, to shake the Soviet economy out of the rut of apathetic stagnation that had gripped it since the mid 1970s. This stagnation or process of 'muddling through down' had led to a widening economic and technological gap between the USSR and the West and threatened the Soviet Union's future position as a superpower. His policy prescription for economic revival was similar in many ways to that of his mentor Andropov, involving the instilling of discipline and enthusiasm and the removal of corruption and black marketeering to make the existing system work better, as well as the introduction of a limited series of pragmatic reforms. For example, as a former regional party boss, he was attracted to the idea of greater economic decentralisation in which factory managers and workers would be freed from stifling local party control and price and wage incentives used in a limited 'Dengist' manner. He sought also to reduce the Soviet Union's growing defence burden by establishing improved relations with the West and China and by effecting new arms control agreements. This would free resources for domestic industrial investment. As a great admirer of the Lenin era, he dreamt, in addition, of re-establishing the CPSU as a popular, respected and effective executive body. He sought to cleanse the party, by removing corrupt, obstructive and incompetent dead wood placemen, and to make it more open and participative.

Gorbachev's Early Record in Power

Gorbachev's economic and foreign policy initiatives will be examined in Parts 3 and 4. In this section attention is focused upon Gorbachev's political reforms, party changes and style of leadership.

The Remoulding of the Politburo and Secretariat   Andrei Gromyko, when putting forward Mikhail Gorbachev's name as party leader to his Politburo colleagues on 10 March 1985, spoke of him as the man who would lead the party into the next millennium. Gorbachev needed, however, to move quickly in the months after March 1985 to consolidate his grip over the levers of power to make his authority meaningful. This he did with alacrity, radically renovating the Politburo and Secretariat during his first year in power as a new 'Gorbachev team' was assembled. He was helped in these efforts by the unusually small size of these inherited bodies and by the rapid aging of his opponents, which removed the need for ruthless and contentious purges.

The first decisive move by Gorbachev to strengthen his power base within the CPSU's ruling councils occurred at the Central Committee plenum of 23 April 1985. Here, using the lower level Central Committee support that he had built up in 1983 as Andropov's oblast campaign manager, he secured the promotion of three technocratic (all are qualified engineers) supporters as full members of the Politburo: the 56-year-old Central Committee Secretary for the economy Nikolai Ryzhkov, the 64-year-old Central Committee Secretary for personnel and ideology Yegor Ligachev, and the 62-year-old KGB chief Viktor Chebrikov. This gave Gorbachev the clear Politburo majority for change which Andropov had lacked.

Two other significant changes were effected during this reshuffle. Firstly, Viktor Nikonov (56), an agronomist who had worked both in the Krasnoyarsk region of Siberia and under Gorbachev as Deputy Minister for Agriculture of the Soviet Union, was brought into the Secretariat to take over the agriculture portfolio. Secondly, Defence Minister Marshal Sergei Sokolov was granted candidate membership of the Politburo. The former change meant that the General Secretary would maintain a close personal interest in agriculture. The latter's promotion, but to a position short of full membership, was an indication that the military lobby would not be granted, under Gorbachev, the prominence it had achieved during the Brezhnev years.

Less than two months later Gorbachev moved decisively to remove his most serious rival within the Politburo, Grigori Romanov, the man who had voted against Gorbachev in the leadership elections of 1984 and 1985 and had spoken unfavourably about him during a recent visit to Hungary. This ousting was carefully organised. It began with KGB-induced stories concerning his arrogant behaviour and drunken, licentious lifestyle, followed by a critical Gorbachev visit to his fiefdom of Leningrad, before Romanov was unceremoniously retired by the Central Committee on 1 July 1985, allegedly on the grounds of 'ill health'. (To appease the feelings of Russia's second largest city, Lev Zaikov, the 61-year-old party leader of Leningrad, was brought into the Central Committee Secretariat to take over the Defence Industry portfolio.)

49

During this 1 July reshuffle Gorbachev promoted an additional close supporter to Politburo membership, Edward Shevardnadze, the 57-year-old Georgian party boss. Shevardnadze, coming from a region adjoining Stavropol, had been a long-time associate of the new party General Secretary. In addition, he had in Georgia, as first Interior Minister and then Party First Secretary, developed a reputation as an upright campaigner against local corruption and as an agricultural innovator. A day later Shevardnadze, surprisingly, replaced Andrei Gromyko as Foreign Minister, the veteran diplomat being moved upstairs to the ceremonial post of State President. This meant that Gorbachev, unlike Brezhnev, Andropov or Chernenko before him, failed, for the time being at least, to combine the two titles of President and CPSU General Secretary. In return for this sacrifice of prestige, however, Gorbachev was able to gain control over foreign affairs, through the removal of the inflexible and outmoded Gromyko.

Two months later, Gorbachev achieved firm control over the state government machine by persuading the aging 80-year-old Brezhnevite, Nikolai Tikhonov, to gracefully step down as Prime Minister on health grounds on 27 September. His departing message spoke warmly of the 'friendly, comradely atmosphere that has been created in the Politburo in recent times'; in return Tikhonov was granted privileged retirement perks. He was replaced by the engineering technocrat Nikolai Ryzhkov whose career had largely been spent in industry and state government management.[1] In addition, the veteran head of Gosplan, Nikolai Baibakov, who had held the post since 1965, was also retired in October 1985, to be replaced by a more dynamic technocrat Nikolai Talyzin (56). Talyzin, a trained telecommunications engineer who had previously served as Minister of Communications, the USSR's Comecon Representative and as a Deputy Premier, was also given a non-voting seat in the Politburo and made First Deputy Prime Minister as an indication of his importance in the economic sphere.

The final member of the Brezhnev old guard to be removed in 1985 was Gorbachev's rival for the General Secretaryship in March 1985, the Moscow party chief Viktor Grishin. He was ousted, like Romanov, following a KGB-inspired newspaper

---

[1] Tikhonov was subsequently relieved of his Politburo seat and Ryzhkov of his Secretariat post at the Central Committee meeting of 15 October 1985.

'whispering campaign' during the autumn of 1985 which was critical of Grishin's complacent mismanagement of the large Moscow municipality, particularly its house construction programme. This campaign culminated on 24 December in Grishin's sacking and replacement as Moscow first secretary by Boris Yeltsin (55), a tough talking former factory manager and party chief of the Sverdlovsk region of Western Siberia who had been brought to Moscow as Central Committee Secretary in charge of construction in July 1985. Yeltsin proceeded, during the spring of 1986, to dismantle Grishin's Moscow machine, replacing mayor Vladimir Promyslov with Valery Saikin (49), the former head of the Likhachev car plant, and purging the municipal party committee and factory leadership cadres. He was to rapidly emerge as one of the strongest supporters of Gorbachev's efficiency, anti-corruption and decentralisation initiatives and became a non-voting candidate member of the Politburo at the Central Committee meeting in February 1986. At this same meeting Grishin was deprived of his Politburo seat.

The final series of Politburo and Secretariat changes effected by Mikhail Gorbachev during his first year in power took place at the end of the 27th CPSU Congress in March 1986 once the new, Gorbachev-orientated, CPSU Central Committee had been elected. One additional member was added to the existing eleven-man Politburo, Lev Zaikov (62), the former fitter, shop foreman and Leningrad party chief who was now in the Secretariat. In addition, two 'candidate' members were added to the Politburo (see Table 3): Yuri Solovyov (61), a former Industrial Construction Minister and the contemporary Leningrad party boss, and Nikolai Slyunkov (57), a former deputy chairman of Gosplan who had been appointed party leader of Byelorussia by Yuri Andropov in January 1983. Both were strong Gorbachev supporters. They replaced the octogenarian Boris Ponomarev and Vasily Kuznetsov who were removed from the body.

In the Secretariat, the changes effected at the 27th Congress were particularly sweeping, five new members being brought into the expanded eleven-member body. The party's two old foreign policy experts, Boris Ponomarev (International Department) and Konstantin Rusakov (Liaison with Socialist Countries), were retired and replaced by Anatoly Dobrynin (67),

---

[1] Ivan Kapitonov (Light Industry), who became chairman of the CPSU's 83-member Central Auditing Commission, was the third member to be removed from the Secretariat in March 1986.

the Soviet Union's former ambassador to Washington, and by Vadim Medvedev (57), a former liaison man for the Central Committee between the CPSU and educational and scientific institutions.[1] They were to work with Alexander Yakovlev (62), Gorbachev's image maker, who was in charge of a new combined culture, propaganda and international department, to provide high-powered foreign policy advice to the new General Secretary. A fourth addition to the new Secretariat was Georgy Razumovsky (50), an agronomist and former obkom secretary from the Krasnodar region bordering Stavropol with whom Gorbachev had previously worked closely. He had been in charge of the Central Committee's cadres department since June 1985. The fifth and final new Secretariat member was a woman, Aleksandra Biryukhova (57), a former trade union official, who was placed in charge of a new Social Affairs department with the brief to tackle the problems of increased crime, juvenile delinquency and divorce and to encourage a return to traditional family norms. She was the first woman to be appointed into such a senior party body since the Khrushchevite Yekaterina Furtseva, who had been a Culture Minister and Politburo member until 1961. Biryukhova's appointment was a populist and progressive move and reflected Gorbachev's concern, influenced by his reformist wife Raisa, to see women more actively involved in Soviet public affairs. (See Appendix B.)

With these changes completed Gorbachev was in a dominant position within the party's controlling bodies, with a clear majority for reform now existing within both the Politburo and Secretariat. Indeed, by March 1986 only two traditional Brezhnevites retained full membership of the Politburo, Vladimir Shcherbitsky and Dinmukhamed Kunayev. They managed to survive widespread purges of their local party machines during the autumn of 1985 and stinging personal criticisms at their republic congresses in January 1986 largely because, as regional chiefs of ethnic stock, they did not represent a direct threat to Gorbachev. In addition, they remained locally popular and influential figures in two large and potentially rebellious border republics and displayed a willingness to adjust their stance and provide support for the new Gorbachev administration: Shcherbitsky indeed had been a supporter of Yuri Andropov's election in November 1982 and a firm opponent of Chernenko.

The new men, and women, now in charge of Soviet affairs were

TABLE 3 : THE CPSU POLITBURO AND SECRETARIAT IN MARCH 1986

POLITBURO

Full Members	Age		Date First Elected
Mikhail Gorbachev	(55)	General Secretary	October 1980
Yegor Ligachev	(65)	Secretariat	April 1985
Nikolai Ryzhkov	(56)	Prime Minister[2]	April 1985
Mikhail Solomentsev	(72)	Chmn Pty Control Cmm[4]	Dec. 1983
Dinmukhamed Kunayev	(74)	1st Secy, Kazakhstan[1]	April 1971[5]
Vladimir Shcherbitsky	(67)	1st Secy, Ukraine Pty[1]	April 1971
Vitaly Vorotnikov	(60)	Russian Federation PM[4]	Dec. 1983
Geidar Aliyev	(63)	Deputy Prime Minister[4]	Nov. 1982
Edward Shevardnadze	(58)	Foreign Minister[3]	July 1985
Andrei Gromyko	(76)	State President	April 1973
Lev Zaikov	(62)	Secretariat[3]	March 1986
Viktor Chebrikov	(62)	KGB Chief[4]	April 1985
Average Age	(64)		

CANDIDATES

Sergei Sokolov	(74)	Defence Minister	July 1985
Yuri Solovyov	(61)	Leningrad Party Chief[3]	March 1986
Nikolai Slyunkov	(56)	Byelorussia Party Leader[4]	March 1986[6]
Nikolai Talyzin	(57)	Head of Gosplan[3]	October 1985
Boris Yeltsin	(55)	Moscow Party Chief[2]	February 1986
Pyotr Demichev	(68)	Culture Minister (till Aug)[1]	November 1964
Vladimir Dolgikh	(61)	Secretariat[1]	May 1982
Average Age	(62)		

SECRETARIAT

Mikhail Gorbachev	(55)	General Secretary	December 1978
Aleksandra Biryukhova	(57)	Social Affairs[3]	March 1986
Anatoly Dobrynin	(66)	Foreign Affairs[3]	March 1986
Vladimir Dolgikh	(61)	Heavy Industry[1]	December 1972
Lev Zaikov	(62)	Defence Industry[3]	July 1985
Mikhail Zimyanin	(72)	Propaganda[1]	December 1978[7]
Yegor Ligachev	(65)	Ideology	December 1983
Vadim Medvedev	(57)	Overseas CP Relations[3]	March 1986
Viktor Nikonov	(57)	Agriculture[3]	April 1985
Georgy Razumovsky	(50)	Organisation[3]	March 1986
Alexander Yakovlev	(62)	Culture/International Dept[3]	March 1986[8]
Average Age	(60)		

[1] Brezhnevite/Romanov Faction   [2] Ligachev Faction   [3] Gorbachev Faction
[4] Andropovite   [5] Removed January 1987
[6] Also brought into the Secretariat in January 1987
[7] Removed January 1987 and place filled by Anatoly Lukyanov (56)
[8] Given, in addition, 'candidate' status in the Politburo in January 1987

a generation younger than the Brezhnev team, being in their fifties and early sixties, and were drawn primarily from technocratic and regional party backgrounds, particularly from the new growth zones of the eastern and southern Soviet Union. In addition, a significant number had worked for the KGB, the political influence of which body was now most significant. The majority of the team (see Table 3) were 'Andropovites', who had been earmarked for high office by the former KGB and party leader. Others — Vorotnikov, Ryzhkov, Yeltsin — were protégés of the influential figure of Andrei Kirilenko who had enjoyed a power base in the Sverdlovsk heavy industry and defence industry region of the Urals and who had boasted a reputation as a tough, but reformist centraliser. This faction became supporters of Andropov as Kirilenko's health deteriorated during the early 1980s. They were led in 1986 by Yegor Ligachev, the second ranking figure in the CPSU, who had served as regional party First Secretary in both the Novosibirsk and Tomsk regions of Siberia, and they dominated the industrial and ideology spheres. These groups supported General Secretary Gorbachev, who had, in addition, his own personal faction of dependent clients who were based primarily in the Secretariat (Biryukhova, Dobrynin, Medvedev, Nikonov, Razumovsky and Yakovlev), Foreign Ministry (Shevardnadze) and Agricultural Ministry (Murakhovsky).

The Purge of Party and Ministerial Personnel   Gorbachev's remoulding of the Politburo and Secretariat was far-reaching and dramatic. Equally sweeping was the anti-corruption and inefficiency campaign which he directed against the upper and middle rungs of the party and state government machines. This campaign, which was co-ordinated by Yegor Ligachev and Georgy Razumovsky, was a continuation of the Andropov purge of 1983 which had resulted in the removal of 19 out of 84 state government ministers and a fifth of the regional party chiefs. The campaign was launched in a vigorous fashion on 24 March 1985, three days after the Politburo had agreed a paper calling for a 'decisive turn in the economy', and was coupled with a major campaign against alcoholism. It was supported, in addition, by a new, more open and critical, style of press reporting, in which readers were encouraged to write in and voice their grievances against incompetent officials, and by a series of high-profile 'anti-inertia tours' by General Secretary Gorbachev.

The first area to fall victim to the purge was Volgograd, where a third of local party officials were dismissed on 25 March. On the same day *Pravda* (the CPSU official organ) attacked the officials of the Bashkin region of the Urals for 'deceiving the state and violating legal and moral norms' and a day later the Ukrainian administration was officially censured. In June 1985, a front page Pravda editorial called for the promotion of more women and young people by local parties and a month later a major anti-corruption drive was launched in Kazakhstan. This ended in the dismissal of the First Secretary of the industrial Chimkent Region, Asanbai Askarov, for falsifying planning figures. The purges gathered pace in the autumn and winter months of 1985 as Ligachev and Razumovsky sought to renovate the CPSU Central Committee in time for the party's February-March 1986 27th Congress. Attention was concentrated in particular upon the notoriously corrupt Central Asian republics, where the party leaders of Turkmenistan, Tadzhikistan and Kirgizia were replaced. In addition, in the key cities of Leningrad and Moscow the new party First Secretaries, Yuri Solovyov and Boris Yeltsin, carried out major middle-ranking reshuffles.

By February 1986 Gorbachev's purge of party cadres had resulted in the replacement of two-thirds of provincial First Party Secretaries, a third of regional chiefs and a fifth of local cadres in total. This meant that at the February-March 1986 CPSU Congress there was a 40% turnover rate in the composition of the new 307-member Central Committee, thus giving the Gorbachev team a firm grip over the party machine — some observers, perhaps overenthusiastically, putting their support at a level of 60-70%. In the state ministries changes were equally sweeping. By February 1986, half of the country's 80 state ministers had been removed, including those responsible for oil, petro-chemicals, iron and steel, light industry, construction, foreign trade and transport.[1] They were replaced by a new generation of technocrat specialists. Similar personnel changes were far-reaching at the factory management level. Finally, in the armed forces and diplomatic service, there was a significant,

[1] A number of senior officials were imprisoned for corruption, for example Viktor Vishnyakov (deputy minister for construction); some middle-ranking apparatchiki, including two foreign trade officials, Smelyakov and Pavlov, were sentenced to death for accepting bribes during the Andropov administration and several corrupt ministers in the Central Asian Republics were executed while many more were expelled from the party. The late Leonid Brezhnev's son-in-law, General Yuri Churbanov (the former deputy minister of the interior), was among those arrested.

though smaller, turnover among leading cadres (see Part 3).[1]

The anti-corruption and anti-inertia campaigns reached a crescendo at the 27th Congress when major speeches were made by Gorbachev, Yeltsin and Aliyev criticising the sloth of the later Brezhnev years and calling for higher standards of conduct among apparatchiks. However, with its immediate objectives achieved, i.e. the replacement of old guard leaders by new, co-operative Gorbachevites, the campaign was gradually tempered during the summer months of 1986. Attention was shifted instead to corruption at the lower levels of the Soviet polity and society, for example, moonlighting and black marketeering.

Gorbachev's Style of Rule and Political Reforms As Gorbachev's control over the party and state bureaucrat machines deepened he became able to introduce new reform initiatives in the economic and diplomatic spheres (see Parts 3 and 4). In the political sphere, the early Gorbachev era has also seen significant developments with respect to the method of governing; the use of the media; culture and ideology; and party organisation.

The most dramatic initial impact made by Mikhail Gorbachev has been in his style of rule. He has provided, in contrast to his three aged, shambling predecessors, a more active and higher profile form of leadership, engaging in major tours overseas and inside the Soviet Union. He has emerged as a compelling and charismatic orator, subtly modulating his tone and moods and skilfully projecting himself to both platform and television audiences. And strikingly, Gorbachev has acted in an open and populist manner, engaging in 'meet the people' walkabouts around factories, schools and hospitals in the key centres of Leningrad, Dnepropetrovsk, Tyumen and Kazakhstan in 1985 and in Khabarovsk and Vladivostok in 1986. During his tours and television appearances he has spoken in a blunt fashion about the urgent need for improved discipline and heightened productivity and has encouraged criticism of ineffective bureaucrats and managers. Typical of such addresses were his demand in Leningrad in May 1985 for anyone not willing to change their attitudes to 'simply get out of our way' and his rebuke to delegates at the 27th CPSU Congress for failing to applaud his criticisms of production inefficiency. This frank and populist style

---

[1] A further significant appointment, though not connected with the anti-corruption campaign, was the replacement of General Vitaly Fedorchuk as minister for Internal Affairs by Alexander Vlasov (formerly First Secretary of the Rostov party committee and a close Caucasus colleague of Gorbachev's) in January 1986.

recalled that of Nikita Khrushchev and was geared towards mobilising public support for change and building up pressure from below on the remaining Brezhnevite bureaucrats. Gorbachev differed, however, from Khrushchev in being a more sophisticated and coolly calculating political operator as well as being supported by a fully developed national television network with which to project his personality.

This television medium has been skilfully used by Gorbachev, who has emerged as the first Soviet leader to copy Western styles of political marketing. His speeches at home, including his 5½-hour address to the 27th CPSU Congress, and abroad, for example his October 1985 Paris press conference, have been given extensive television coverage. In his well-cut Savile Row suits Gorbachev, with his attractive wife Raisa, has presented himself in a modern presidential fashion. By refusing to aggrandise the posts of President or Prime Minister and by calling upon Pravda to use quotes from Lenin rather than himself in leading articles, he appears to be seeking to build a unique new 'anti-personality' cult and to present himself as a no-nonsense leader concerned more with results than with personal praise. In addition, Gorbachev has spoken on a number of occasions of his desire to effect a return to a more genuinely Leninist style of collectivist rule within the Politburo. In reality, however, Gorbachev has developed his own powerful 'Kremlin office' advisory team, grouped around the figures of Alexander Yakovlev, Anatoly Dobrynin, Yevgeny Velikhov (scientific adviser) and Professor Abel Agenbegyan (economics adviser), and shows signs of governing in an increasingly direct manner. Such a return to a more personalised form of rule would be popular among many sections of Soviet society and would accord with Russian traditions.

In the cultural and ideological sphere, Gorbachev's first year in power has seen a halting 'thaw' and relaxation of censorship as the General Secretary has sought to instigate a wide-ranging policy debate and win the support of intellectuals for his new economic programme. Changes have been most striking, as has been noted, in the state-controlled newspaper and television media where there has been a marked departure from traditional dull and smug optimistic reporting towards greater frankness, realism and openness (*glasnost*). In Pravda, openly critical letters, drawing attention to apparatchik privileges, cadre corruption and shoddy consumer goods, have been extensively published, while on the state television, under a new chief, Alexander Aksyonov since April

1986, reporting has been revamped to include previously taboo subjects such as Soviet earthquake and flood disasters, drug taking and military casualties in Afghanistan. This change in style became most clearly evident following the Chernobyl nuclear reactor disaster of April 1986, when, after an initial period of media silence, extensive television coverage was given, drawing attention to the magnitude of the catastrophe and the mistakes made.[1]

In the arts, both Mikhail Gorbachev and his wife Raisa have emerged as interested patrons and connoisseurs, encouraging greater liveliness and innovation. Despite the continuance of KGB crackdowns against internal dissidents and the statement made by Mikhail Gorbachev at the 27th Party Congress that 'only a literature that is ideologically motivated' would be acceptable, there has been a perceptible loosening of pettifogging state interference in cultural affairs. A number of previously blacklisted poets, for example Yevgeny Yevtushenko, a strong critic of the Stalin and Brezhnev eras, have been rehabilitated and given official support, while controversial subjects, such as Jewish emigration, have begun to be covered in approved plays. In addition, former hardline culture officials, including the Culture Minister Pyotr Demichev, the State Publishing Committee (SPC) chairman Boris Pashtukov, the Soviet Writers' Union (SWU) president Georgy Markov and the Soviet Filmmakers' Union (SFU) president Lev Kulidzhanov, have been ousted and replaced by more reformist figures. The Glavlit state censorship body has been disbanded.[2]

In the field of party ideology and organisation, Mikhail Gorbachev, remembering the fate of the impetuous Nikita Khrushchev, has been more cautious. A new, revised and updated edition of the CPSU's Third (1961) Party Programme was adopted by the 27th Congress on 1 March 1986, but it contained few ideological

[1] The public responded favourably to this change in content and style, Soviet newspaper circulation rising by more than 14 million between March 1985 and December 1986, while television output and audiences also increased significantly.

[2] At the head of the SPC now is Mikhail Nenashev (formerly editor of the pioneeringly frank newspaper 'Sovietskaya Rossiya'), the SWU, Vladimir Karpov (former editor of the literary magazine 'Novy Mir'), and the SFU, the controversial film director Elem Klimov. The new Minister of Culture is Vasily Zakharov (formerly the deputy head of the CPSU Central Committee's Propaganda Department). Pyotr Demichev has been 'moved upstairs', being appointed first deputy chairman of the Praesidium of the Supreme Soviet (i.e. state vice-president) in June 1986.

innovations. It concentrated primarily on economic and international affairs in a typically pragmatic and down-to-earth Gorbachevian fashion, remained vague concerning the date at which the Soviet Union would move from socialism to 'full communism', and continued to uphold the nebulous Brezhnevite concept of 'developed socialism'. There have been, however, subtle and significant innovations in Gorbachev's approach to party organisation and rules.

In his address to the 27th Congress, Gorbachev stated that during the previous quinquennium CPSU membership had grown by 1.6 million to a total of 19 million (6.8% of the population) and remarked that, in future, the growth in membership should be slowed and that greater attention be paid when recruiting members to skills, ability and commitment. He criticised time-serving 'careerists' within party ranks who 'just play to go along with reorganisation' and who are unwilling to take on responsibility, and he called for the promotion of greater internal party democracy and self-criticism. Taken together, these comments suggested a wish to return the CPSU to its early Leninist model of a small, upright, respected, enlightened and intellectual body providing strategic leadership to the nation and acting as an example to those outside. In addition, Gorbachev sought to transform party officials from being what he termed cautious, inert and formal 'armchair managers' into creative, innovative and enterprising leaders.

In achieving this aim of remoulding the CPSU, the 1985-86 anti-corruption and anti-inertia drive has formed an essential initial step. It has been followed at the 27th Congress by the introduction of two significant new rule changes. In the first, party committees at all levels were mandated to report their work in responding to criticisms made by individual members, thus preventing ruling committees from gagging complaints. In the second, party members were made personally responsible for tasks assigned to them and became no longer able to hide themselves under the umbrella of 'collective leadership' when mistakes were made. Gorbachev, keenly aware of apparatchiki opposition, has shied away from a third, more fundamental, rule change on Khrushchev's Rule 25 model, in which restrictions would be placed on office tenure and forced rotation introduced, preferring to rely on the removal of ineffective officials through the indirect process of media and central party criticism. At the Central Committee Plenum held immediately after the 1986 27th Congress, however, he gave notification that the 'cadres issue' would be placed at the head of the agenda for their next scheduled meeting in September 1986.

The succeeding months were consumed with concealed in-fighting between radical and 'gradualist' reformist factions over the desirable pace of change. Gorbachev, supported in the Politburo by the assertive Boris Yeltsin and in the press by economists, academicians and columnists, including Izvestiya's Alexander Bovin, assumed leadership of the radical wing of the ruling élite. He was opposed, however, not just by regional and republic level conservative Brezhnevites, but also by a more powerful and senior group of 'gradualist' and centralist reformers led by Yegor Ligachev and Prime Minister Ryzhkov. This opposition forced the postpone-ment of the proposed session of the CPSU Central Committee in September 1986, in a month during which rumours of an assassin-ation attempt on the Gorbachevs during their July 1986 visit to Vladivostok circulated through Moscow.

Gorbachev quickly made clear his dominance, however, through a number of dramatic new moves in the autumn and winter of 1986-87. In October 1986, the party leader launched a major new arms reduction initiative at the US-USSR 'mini-summit' at Reykjavik, which was followed by a remarkably successful diplomatic offensive directed towards Western Europe. Then, on 16 Decem-ber 1986, Gorbachev finally succeeded in ousting Dinmukhamed Kunayev as party first secretary in Kazakhstan, replacing him with a 'Great Russian', Gennady Kolbin[1], in a move which provoked immediate and violent Kazakh nationalist riots in the republic capital of Alma-Ata. Seven days later, the Soviet Union's most prominent dissident, Andrei Sakharov, was released from internal exile in the closed city of Gorky, as a new drive towards cultural liberalisation was now launched (see Part 5).

These initiatives were indicative of mounting success for the Gorbachev faction in the intra-élite power struggle and paved the way for the convocation of the postponed plenary meeting of the CPSU Central Committee on 27-28 January 1987. At this key plenum, Kunayev was formally removed from the Politburo, while the party leader gained the promotion of three further supporters into the senior organs of the party. Alexander Yakovlev, the party's Culture Secretary, was inducted into the Politburo as a 'candidate' member.

---

[1] Kolbin (59), who had attended the same Sverdlovsk polytechnic as Prime Minister Ryzhkov and Boris Yeltsin and who had served as deputy to Edward Shevardnadze in Georgia during the mid 1970s, enjoyed a reputation as a strict disciplinarian and corruption fighter. He became the only republic first secretary not to be drawn from among the local ethnic community.

Nikolai Slyunkov, the reformist Byelorussia party first secretary and already a Politburo 'candidate', was given a seat in the further expanded twelve-member Secretariat. Finally, Gorbachev's old Moscow University law student friend, Anatoly Lukyanov (56), who had been working within the Secretariat's crucial general administrative department, was also made a full party Secretary, replacing Mikhail Zimyanin, who was retired on health grounds. Gorbachev failed in this reshuffle to remove Vladimir Shcherbitsky, the last remaining true Brezhnevite within the Politburo, or to significantly change the voting balance between radicals and gradualists. He did, however, further strengthen his hold over the party's policy framing Secretariat.

The most striking element of the January 1987 Central Committee plenum was not, however, the personnel changes effected, but rather the party General Secretary's call, during a monumental 130-page speech which, unusually, was immediately published after the meeting by TASS. He called for a movement towards real 'socialist democracy' within both the party and state channels of government through the introduction of new institutional reforms. While making it clear that he was not seeking to undermine the principle of 'democratic centralism', Gorbachev proposed a significant extension of inner party participation through the upgrading of the role of party meetings and committees and called for the injection of an element of competition (between acceptable candidates) into selection for party posts. Experiments with such competition had already been made at the local level. Now, Gorbachev gave his formal support to the use of competitive secret ballot elections for party posts up to the republic first secretary level, for state soviets and for senior factory and commune executive positions, emulating, in many respects, the system employed in neighbouring Poland and Hungary. In addition, Gorbachev called for the promotion of skilled non-party members into senior state positions and for a continuance of the glasnost campaign, suggesting the passage of a new law that would allow Soviet citizens to be immune from retribution for criticisms made concerning the party or their employers. In proposing these reforms, the party leader reassured anxious and unenthusiastic conservative members of the Central Committee that the pace of change would be gradual and that strict 'discipline' and 'responsibility' would be maintained. In addition, provision was made for a more extended and extensive discussion of the proposals in a special 'All Union Party Congress', the first since 1941, which

61

Gorbachev announced would be convened in Moscow in 1988 to debate and rule on the 'cadres issue'.

Taken together, Gorbachev's personnel changes and new policy initiatives represent a significant change in course for the Soviet polity. In his address to the 27th CPSU Congress Gorbachev spoke of the Soviet Union standing at 'an abrupt turning point' in the nation's history in which 'obsolescent social patterns and the style and methods of work' would need to be radically changed and updated. At the crucial Central Committee plenum of January 1987, after castigating Stalin and Brezhnev's 'simplistic' perversion of true Leninist teachings, he further stressed the need for far-reaching institutional change, extending accountability and participation, if economic reconstruction (*perestroika*) was to be achieved. Such a revolution in attitudes, organisation and behaviour is gradually being effected in both the political and economic spheres (see Part 4). Particularly sweeping and breathtaking has been the change-over of personnel and the transformation in the style of rule. With regard to substantive reforms, however, Gorbachev has necessarily been more cautious. He has needed to act at a pace which will not lead to revolt either by the Soviet generals or by more cautious and centralising reformers within the Politburo and Central Committee grouped around the figure of Yegor Ligachev. Such constraints facing the new General Secretary are explored in greater detail in Parts 3 and 4.

62

Part Three

DEFENCE AND FOREIGN POLICIES

The 1970s: The Decade of Détente

During the two decades following the 1945 Yalta Summit, East-West relations deteriorated alarmingly as the West, smarting over the Soviet perfidy which had gained them dominance over Eastern Europe, restricted economic and diplomatic contacts. Russia's suppression of the populist uprisings in Hungary (1956) and Czechoslovakia (1968), its clandestine involvement with anti-imperial 'freedom fighting' movements in Africa and Asia during the 1950s and 1960s, and its support for Fidel Castro's Cuban revolution in 1959, only served to further sour international relations during this 'Cold War' era. The erection of the Berlin wall in 1961 and the Cuban missile crisis of 1962 marked the low point for these relations.

From the mid 1960s, however, Alexei Kosygin, the Soviet Prime Minister, began to argue in favour of improved East-West relations for economic reasons. Increased East-West trade and access to sophisticated Western technology could, Kosygin argued, be used as a policy substitute for genuine domestic economic reform at low ideological cost. The West in turn (particularly Western Europe) was anxious to reduce military spending, to increase markets for its manufactures and food surpluses, to secure additional supply resources for raw materials and minerals and to tame further Soviet expansion. These ideas were taken up by Leonid Brezhnev and by Presidents Nixon, Ford and Chancellors Brandt and Schmidt during the 1970s. The decade of détente encompassed the Strategic Arms Limitation Treaty (SALT) I (1972), the Anti-Ballistic Missile (ABM) Treaty (1972), the Nuclear Non-Aggression Agreement (1973), the Vladivostok Accords (1974), the Helsinki Final Agreement (1975) and the SALT II negotiations of 1976-79.

However, the Soviet Union, with its experienced, but suspicious, Foreign Minister, Andrei Gromyko, asserting progressively more influence over policy formation, remained most calculating in its pursuance of and adherence to détente. A number of concessions were made to the West, such as the temporary relaxation of Jewish emigration restrictions, but the Soviet military arms build-up continued apace during this decade, and its foreign and defence ministries did not hesitate from forcefully pushing forward Soviet interests when opportunities presented themselves. Major openings for the Soviet Union arose in particular between 1975 and 1980. The weakness and introspection of an American regime, scarred by the defeat in Vietnam and the impeachment of its President, and the collapse of the Portuguese empire following the 1974-75 revolution, allowed Russia to gain significant bases in Angola and Mozambique in Africa, as well as in South Yemen and Ethiopia in the Gulf zone. The Soviet Union (with Cuba) also furthered the interests of the Sandinistas in Nicaragua and supported its Vietnamese allies in the *anschluss* of Laos and Kampuchea.

The 1970s thus represented a decade during which the Soviet Union emerged as a commanding and internationally recognised superpower with a powerful voice around the conference tables of the world. Its global interests were extending and deepening, particularly in Africa and Southeast Asia. Relations with China on its eastern frontiers became strained by events in Vietnam, but relations with Europe and America were thawing as economic and diplomatic contact increased. Three events between 1979 and 1981 were to dramatically undermine this cosy development of détente and to once more plunge the Soviet Union and the United States into a renewal of 'cold war' rhetoric: the overthrow of the Shah of Iran (1978-79), the Soviet invasion of Afghanistan (December 1979), and the growth and subsequent repression of the Solidarity free trade union movement in Poland (1980-81).

Foreign Policy During Brezhnev's Final Years: 1978-1982

The June 1979 summit meeting held between Leonid Brezhnev and President Carter, which was concluded by the signature of SALT II, marked the closing chapter in the era of détente and cordial Soviet-American relations. The US President had begun his term in office (1977-80) pursuing a 'new American foreign policy' based upon freedom from the 'inordinate fear of communism' which had in the past compelled the United States to embrace all manner of anti-Soviet dictators. America's new foreign policy was now concerned above all with human rights and sought to foster economic and political development in the Third World. This policy, however, met with fierce criticism from conservative circles in the United States as Soviet military spending, which had reached parity with the US in 1971, continued to grow by 3-5% per annum (in real terms) during the 1970s, while US spending declined, and as portions of Africa and Asia continued to be brought into the Soviet 'sphere of influence'. It took the overthrow of the Shah of Iran, an American ally in a key oil-rich region, by Shi'ite fundamentalists in 1978-79, the subsequent capture and confinement of American hostages in the US Embassy in Teheran (November 1979 — January 1981), and the Soviet invasion of Afghanistan during the Christmas of 1979 to effect a sea-change in American opinion which was to sound a death knell to 1970s détente.

The Afghanistan Invasion

The immediate pretext for the Soviet invasion of Afghanistan was the need to secure in power, following the so-called 'Brezhnev doctrine,' the client Marxist regime which had been established by a coup in 1978. Russia had recently signed a friendship and co-operation treaty with that regime, but now it faced opposition from Islamic tribal guerrillas. This client regime had provided the Russians with a useful military base within fighter plane reach of the oil states of the Middle East. A secondary consideration was the importance of securing Afghanistan as a reliable buffer state on Russia's southern borders and to prevent the spread of Islamic revivalism into Turkestan, an increasingly important demographic and economic region within the Soviet Union. Thus the two principal directives of Soviet policy, a defensive concern for security and an aggressive desire to 'give history a push', were combined in the Afghanistan invasion.

It is clear, however, that sanction for such an action, which would have serious international repercussions, would not have been forthcoming unless there had been important changes within the Soviet policy-making power structure and in foreign policy perceptions which gave the upper hand to more 'hawkish' groupings. Such changes did occur, with the voice of the military becoming much stronger within the Politburo and the key executive organs during the closing years of the 1970s. This military lobby favoured the use of Russia's new military muscle in pursuance of its foreign policy objectives. This view gained broader support among less hawkish policy makers as it became clear during the final months of 1979 that the US Senate — with a third of its members facing re-election in 1980 — was almost certain to dismember or reject the SALT II agreement and that the 1980 presidential elections would return a conservative Republican leader, Ronald Reagan. The decision to invade Afghanistan was thus taken in the knowledge that a deterioration in East-West relations and a Western arms build-up would ensue. But such developments appeared inevitable to Soviet policy makers, whether Afghanistan was occupied or not.

The repercussions of the Afghanistan invasion proved, however, in hindsight to be even more far-reaching than Soviet leaders had anticipated. Firstly, victory in the military campaign against Afghan mujaheddin rebels, supplied with Chinese and American arms, was not as quick and decisive as had been expected. Russian troops were able to gain control of urban centres, but were faced with guerrilla resistance in the countryside. Eight years later this guerrilla warfare had accounted for more than 50 000 Soviet casualties and was continuing to tie up more than 100 000 Soviet troops and impose a mounting economic burden on the Soviet regime. Secondly, the Afghanistan campaign lost Russia friends in the Islamic world, among the Third World and Non-Aligned community and contributed substantially to a further deterioration in relations with China, pushing the latter power closer to the United States. Thirdly, the Afghanistan invasion brought in its wake Western sanctions — a temporary US grain and high-technology export embargo and a partial Western boycott of the 1980 Moscow Olympics, followed by the collapse of the SALT II agreement and the start of a Western arms build-up. A US rapid-deployment force was set up to police the Persian Gulf; NATO Defence Ministers agreed to increase their military budgets by at least 3% per annum (in real terms) between 1980 and 1986; and plans were made to deploy Pershing-II and Cruise intermediate ballistic missiles (IBMs) in Western Europe to counter Russian SS-20s. In the United States a new right-wing anti-Soviet President, Ronald Reagan, was elected in the winter of 1980 determined to build up

American military strength, pursue an aggressive foreign policy and to halt and wherever possible reverse communist encroachment.

Soviet Foreign Policy Goals for the 1980s

The Soviet Union had by 1980 reached a position of great military and strategic strength. It had become the foremost nuclear and military power in the world and had developed, under Admiral Gorshkov, the world's second largest and most powerful navy to extend the range of its global interests. All this had been achieved on the back of a rickety and sluggish domestic economy through giving priority to military and heavy industry spending over the needs of the consumer sector: by 1980 military spending was taking up between 11-15% of Russian GDP, compared with only 5.2% in the USA, 4.9% in Britain, 4% in France and 3.3% in West Germany. There were signs in 1980, however, that the Soviet Union was becoming overextended, overcommitted to the military sector and becoming dangerously isolated. The huge size of the Soviet Union meant that its military planners, forever fearing 'encirclement', had to maintain large troop and missile contingents in Central Asia and in the Far East on the Afghan and Chinese fronts, in addition to large deployments in Central Europe. It had few firm allies outside of the Warsaw Pact, in contrast with America which could draw upon support from Western Europe, Oceania and East Asia, putting together a coalition which could outnumber the fragmented Soviet forces. Finally, the Russian population growth rate was stagnating, thus promising to produce serious manpower shortages during future decades. The 1970s had been a superficially successful decade for the Soviet Union overseas. The 1980s would be a far more difficult decade as Russia sought to consolidate and continue its advances during a period of Western arms modernisation and re-equipment.

In such circumstances, Soviet foreign policy goals during the 1980s were to be three-pronged. Firstly, Russia would seek to strengthen its global interests by effecting co-operation and friendship treaties with and gaining military bases in sympathetic states. Already by 1980 Cuba, Vietnam, North Korea, Afghanistan and South Yemen provided such support and bases in Central America, East Asia and the Persian Gulf, receiving in return substantial financial subsidies, and in October of that year a 20-year friendship treaty was signed with Syria to secure for the Soviet Union a firmer foothold in the Middle East. Secondly, Russia would attempt to detach China from its closening alliance with the United States and Japan and would attempt to drive a wedge between the United States and its Western European NATO allies. It would stress the 'divisibility of détente', utilising the carrot of expanding East-West trade and future access to Russian mineral and fuel supplies as well as the stick of Soviet military muscle to prise Europe and America apart. An attempt would be made to make Western Europe dependent on the USSR for its energy supplies and thus neutralise or 'Finlandise' this bloc. Thirdly, Russia would seek to place some ceiling upon rising military expenditure by entering into new arms control agreements with America, without sacrificing Soviet superiority. This would free resources for the civilian economy and allow consumer incomes to increase, providing a firmer material base to the Soviet regime. These last two foreign policy aims were, however, doomed to failure by the invasion of Afghanistan and by Soviet reactions to the rise of the Solidarity free trade union movement in Poland in 1980-81.[1]

Foreign Policy Results: 1978-82

China   Talks on the 'normalisation' of Sino-Soviet relations were reopened in the autumn of 1979, but were suspended in January 1980 after events in Kabul led to a further worsening in relations.

   United States   Relations with the United States reached their lowest point since 1962 as the US pursued its nuclear modernisation programme, as arms control talks came to a halt and as diplomatic contact was reduced to a minimum. Soviet military manoeuvres on the Polish borders in 1981, the pressure the USSR imposed upon the Polish premier Kania to take a firm line on the Solidarity movement and the imposition of martial law in December 1981, had a profound effect upon the United States

[1]   This movement came to birth after a series of strikes during the summer of 1980 following acute food shortages. The Solidarity trade union challenged the 'leading role' of the Polish Communist party, forced a number of political concessions from the government (including the right to strike) and threatened to completely break up and supersede the ruling party before Polish troops declared martial law in December 1981 and General Jaruzelski was installed in power.

with its large and vocal Polish community. New economic sanctions were now imposed against the Soviet Union and Poland and further justification was gained for the American arms build-up.

Western Europe It was only in Western Europe that Soviet foreign policy objectives met with limited, though equivocal, success. Here the issue of US nuclear arms modernisation and the proposed installation of 464 Cruise and 108 Pershing-II IBMs on European soil was exploited by the Soviet Union. In October 1979 Leonid Brezhnev denounced this US missile programme as an act of aggression and offered to withdraw small numbers of Soviet tanks and troops from East Germany and to place a ceiling on Soviet medium-range missile numbers, provided that NATO did not go ahead with its deployment plans. In September 1981, during a period when the European peace movement was gaining increasing popular support, Brezhnev made a similar offer to a Labour Party delegation in Moscow.

The issue of East-West trade sanctions was similarly exploited by the Soviet Union during the period between 1980-82 when, with differing economic interests and during a period of severe recession, Western unity frequently broke down. The 1980 grain embargo on the Soviet Union was quickly shattered by huge Argentinian shipments and by the Mid-West farmers' lobby, who with huge unsold surpluses accumulating, persuaded President Reagan to lift restrictions in April 1981. It was, however, the continental nations of France and Germany — the former inheriting a Gaullist independence in foreign policy matters: the latter developing a new anti-Americanism — which proved to be the weakest links in the chain of Western sanctions solidarity. Both nations had important trading relations with Eastern Europe and both, being deficient in energy supplies, sought to gain access to Russian gas through a proposed new pipeline during the 1980s. West Germany with its lingering interest in an eventual reunification of the two Germanies, was particularly keen, following the Brandt-Schmidt policy of Ostpolitik, to maintain channels of communication between East and West and to maintain 1970s détente. Thus during the winter of 1980 a Franco-German consortium broke the Western high-technology trade embargo and supplied parts for a major Russian aluminium project. During the following year a huge $15 billion pipeline equipment deal was effected with a West German-East European consortium in return for future low-cost gas supplies. This prompted retaliatory US sanctions against European companies and a brief falling out between the NATO allies.

However, despite the emergence of these temporary divisions, the Soviet attempt to decouple NATO and block Cruise and Pershing-II deployment proved ultimately to be a failure. Russia's heavy-handed propaganda effort backfired and contributed instead to the election in 1983 of the conservative governments of Margaret Thatcher and Helmut Kohl in Britain and West Germany committed to the installation of these new IBMs.

Foreign Policy Under Andropov and Chernenko: 1982-1985

Relations with the West

The years of 1980 and 1981 marked a low point for East-West relations. But by the time of the death of Leonid Brezhnev in November 1982, a thaw was clearly evident. It was signalled by the easing of Western economic sanctions and the reopening in Geneva of Euromissile and long range nuclear weapons control negotiations with the United States under the title of START (Strategic Arms Reduction Talks). Such an improvement in relations was, however, only to be temporary.

The Soviet Union concentrated in 1983 on a last desperate attempt, through a number of arms reduction offers and a media campaign orchestrated by Yuri Andropov, to persuade the West German parliament to vote against the deployment of the first batch of American Pershing-II missiles on German soil. This 'peace offensive' included an offer in December 1982 by Yuri Andropov, in response to President Reagan's November 1981 'zero option' of full Soviet IBM dismantlement, for a reduction in Soviet SS-4 and SS-20 numbers in Europe from 600 to 150, a figure equivalent to the number of British and French IBMs, provided that Cruise and Pershing-II were not deployed. Soviet hopes of an accommodation were, however, scuppered by the shooting down, with the loss of 269 lives (including one US Congressman), on 1 September 1983, of a South Korean passenger airliner, which had strayed into Russian airspace. The British government began deploying American Cruise missiles during the second week of November 1983 and on 22 November the West German parliament voted to accept Pershing-II. Soviet hopes of preventing the deployment of these new medium-range nuclear missiles had finally ended and on 23 November 1983 the Russian delegation angrily walked out of the Geneva arms talks and began deploying further SS-20 and shorter-range SS-22 missiles in the Soviet Union, Czechoslovakia and East Germany.

During 1984, following these missile deployments and with the accession of the insular-minded Konstantin Chernenko, Soviet-US relations deteriorated once more, reaching their lowest point since Afghanistan. The Russians had exerted considerable self-restraint during the previous two years as the United States became deeply involved in Lebanon and Central America (intervening militarily in Grenada in October 1983) and as South Africa imposed peace treaties on Angola and Mozambique. However, a battle of words was already clearly evident during 1983 as Andrei Gromyko described the United States as 'compulsive gamblers and adventurists' (January 1983), and as Ronald Reagan spoke of the USSR as an 'evil empire' (March 1983). Andrei Gromyko and Dmitri Ustinov, both hardliners, now firmly dominated foreign affairs during this 'cold war' period. Diplomatic contacts were reduced to a frosty minimum, the USSR and much of the Eastern Bloc boycotted the 1984 Los Angeles Olympic Games, and Defence Minister Marshal Ustinov accused the United States of seeking world domination; while on the American side, Ronald Reagan took the opportunity of the D-Day commemoration to criticise the post-war division of Europe and joked during an election campaign aside about bombing the USSR. It was left to European foreign ministers to maintain a bridge between the two superpowers.

Only during the closing months of 1984, when a landslide electoral victory for Ronald Reagan appeared certain, did Soviet policy makers once more realise the need to deal with the US administration and to seek some improvement in relations and some mutual limitations on burdensome military spending. Thus Andrei Gromyko met President Reagan in Washington on 28 September 1984 and arrangements were made for a new round of Geneva arms control meetings to open in March 1985.

Relations with Eastern Europe and China

The efforts of Yuri Andropov, with his 1954-67 Ambassadorship, Central Committee and Secretariat experience of East European and Asian affairs, were more successful in improving Soviet relations with the communist blocs of Eastern Europe and China, than with the West.

In Eastern Europe, the grip of the Soviet Union and the Communist Party over Poland was tightened during these years as the Solidarity movement was muzzled and skilfully brought under state control. Elsewhere in Eastern Europe, economic exigency imposed by the harsh economic climate of the early 1980s forced the Comecon countries into greater dependence upon the Soviet Union for their fuel supplies, credit and markets. The Soviet Union was thus in a position in September 1984 to put pressure on the East German premier, Erich Honecker, to cancel a proposed meeting with the West German Chancellor Helmut Kohl that had been intended as a further step on the path towards German reconciliation.

In the case of China, where a new, more flexible, post-Mao leadership was in power, a determined Soviet drive for rapprochement was signalled by Leonid Brezhnev in his speeches in Tashkent and Baku in March and September 1982. In October 1982, Sino-Soviet negotiations were resumed once more after a three-year break and they gained a further push with Yuri Andropov's reference to 'our great neighbour' in a speech soon after his accession to the General Secretaryship. The Soviet presence in Afghanistan and its support of Vietnam, and China's desire to improve its trading relations with the United States and Japan, remained stumbling blocks to full reconciliation. However, tensions between the two great communist powers did begin to ease significantly from 1982.

Foreign Policy Under Gorbachev

US-Soviet Relations

Mikhail Gorbachev, during his tour of Europe in 1984, had impressed Western leaders as a cultivated, flexible man with whom, in the words of Margaret Thatcher, 'we can do business'. He came to power concerned to continue many of the foreign policy initiatives of his mentor Yuri Andropov — bringing to heel Russia's Eastern European partners, attempting to split Western Europe from the United States and endeavouring to improve Sino-Soviet relations. Gorbachev also, however, was determined, placing as he did top priority upon domestic economic recovery, to prevent an escalation in the arms race spiral which might force his administration to divert critical funds away from the civilian sector. His most important foreign policy concern was to improve and stabilise relations with the United States, to negotiate a new series of arms control agreements and to regain Soviet access to Western high technology and economic markets.

In pursuance of this aim, Gorbachev embarked upon a major new dual-pronged 'peace offensive' from the spring of 1985. Firstly, he sought progress in the arms control negotiations which commenced in Geneva on 12 March and put forward the idea of an autumn summit with President Reagan. Secondly, he launched a series of skilful and eye-catching arms reduction initiatives in a new high profile, media-wise manner. These initiatives were serious in intent but were also of propaganda value, being aimed at the Reagan administration as well as at European public opinion and the Dutch parliament, which was still deciding whether or not to accept 48 American Cruise missiles. In addition, they were geared towards building up opposition within liberal circles in America and Europe against President Reagan's controversial Strategic Defence Initiative (SDI), an advanced high-technology space-based programme which the Soviet Union feared being unable to match.[1]

Gorbachev's first major 'peace initiative' was launched in April 1985 when he advocated a moratorium on the deployment of medium-range nuclear missiles in Europe and offered to make 25% cuts in the Soviet strategic missile armoury if America abandoned the SDI. It gained momentum during the summer of 1985 as preparations were made for a superpower summit to be held in November. Gorbachev, supported by his new and more effusive Foreign Minister, Edward Shevardnadze, and by a radically transformed Soviet diplomatic and public relations team, launched a major propaganda 'media blitz'. This included the opening of a 'Peace and Friendship' World Youth Festival in Moscow and the announcement,on the 30th anniversary of the dropping of the American atomic bomb at Hiroshima (6 August),

---

[1] This 'Star Wars' programme, which was first unveiled by President Reagan in March 1983, aims to create a defensive shield in space against nuclear missiles. The USSR fears, however, that such a shield could be transformed into an offensive 'first strike' weapon.

of the imposition of a unilateral Soviet five-month moratorium on the testing of nuclear missiles and a call for the 'de-militarisation of outer space'. Two months later, Gorbachev made a striking personal impact with a high profile visit to Paris (2-5 October), during which he unveiled a radical new arms offer which envisaged a 50% mutual reduction in Soviet and American strategic nuclear forces, the scrapping of SDI, a moratorium on the deployment of intermediate nuclear forces (INFs) in Europe and the opening of negotiations with France and Britain to seek nuclear parity in Europe.

These arms reduction and test-ban proposals were rejected by an American administration which was committed to continuance of the SDI programme and was seeking to regain nuclear superiority over the USSR. This gave the propaganda initiative to Mikhail Gorbachev, who appeared able to out-communicate the 'Great Communicator' Ronald Reagan himself. The stark differences in both sides' position on the continuance of SDI meant, however, that the November 1985 Geneva Summit failed to achieve anything substantive with respect to arms control. Only minor diplomatic concessions in the cultural exchange sphere were effected, with both sides agreeing, in addition, to hold further summits in 1986 and 1987 in Washington and Moscow.

The failure to achieve major results in Geneva came as a blow to Mikhail Gorbachev and strengthened the position of hawkish groupings at home in the run-up to the February-March 1986 CPSU Congress. Gorbachev continued, however, to press for a 'new détente' in the spring and summer months of 1986. He extended the USSR's unilateral nuclear test-ban three times in January, March and April 1986 and announced major new conventional and nuclear arms reduction initiatives in January and April. These proposals included a utopian scheme for a three-staged elimination of all global nuclear weapons by the year 2000 which incorporated elements of President Reagan's 1981 'zero option'. Once more, however, it was rejected by the United States since it was tied to the abandonment of SDI.

During April and May 1986 Soviet-American relations deteriorated sharply. The Reagan administration launched an anti-terrorist air strike against the USSR's ally Libya and made public its intentions to breach the limits of the SALT II treaty in 1987. These actions made the prospect of arms control agreement increasingly remote. In June 1986, however, Mikhail

Gorbachev unveiled a major new arms reduction proposal which included significant new concessions. It accepted continuance of laboratory research on the SDI project but called for America to continue to abide by the 1972 ABM treaty for a further 15-20 years, thus preventing actual SDI deployment. In return, it offered 30-50% strategic force cuts. In addition, the Gorbachev team put forward a new INF compromise deal which ignored French and British missile forces and proposed the reduction of US and USSR INF missile numbers to a token level of 100 (which would include those in Soviet Asia). Two months later he extended Russia's nuclear test-ban for a further five months and loosened Soviet restrictions on verification procedures. A month later, in September 1986, a Warsaw Pact-NATO conventional force 'confidence building treaty' was signed in Stockholm and agreement was made to hold a preparatory mini-summit in Reykjavik on 11-12 October.

At the Reykjavik mini-summit the Gorbachev team surprised the American team, which had come primarily for an informal ice-breaking meeting to prepare the ground for a subsequent formal summit in Washington, by unveiling a further substantial arms reduction initiative comprising a staggered, cross-board 50% cut in strategic missile forces and the elimination of all superpower INFs in Europe (the 'zero option') within a five-year timespan. The offer, which was later described by the American President as the 'most far-reaching arms-control proposal in history', was seriously considered by the US Reykjavik team, with a special additional fourth negotiating session being convened on the afternoon of Sunday 12 October. It was finally rejected, however, when Soviet negotiators insisted that any agreement should be linked to a US pledge to confine its research on SDI to the laboratory, with no testing or deployment.

The collapse of the Reykjavik summit on the SDI issue threatened to seriously sour Soviet-American relations and usher in a renewed 'cold war' era, with the Gorbachev team being forced to await the outcome of the November 1988 presidential election in the hope that a new US President would be more willing to negotiate an arms reduction agreement. However, two events in the autumn of 1986 significantly changed the climate of opinion within the United States and made the prospects of an arms deal before 1989 a feasible proposition. First, at the US midterm Congressional elections in November 1986, President Reagan, who had already encountered growing pressure from

Politics in the Soviet Union

within Congress during the 1985-86 session for economies in the
defence budget and for the imposition of a nuclear freeze or
test-ban, saw his Republican Party lose control over the Senate.
This setback, with the chairmanship of all Senate committees
including the powerful Foreign Relations Committee now falling
into Democrat hands, was followed almost immediately by the
eruption of what became termed the 'Iran-Contragate' scandal
involving the secret US trading of arms for hostages with Iran and
the Reagan administration's illegal funding of anti-communist
Contra guerrillas in Nicaragua. The scandal, which entailed
breaches of Congressional laws as well as the administration's
stated war against terrorism and which called attention to the
existence of a separate covert foreign policy network, eroded
public confidence in President Reagan, leading to a widespread
questioning of his control over foreign affairs and resulting in the
enforced resignation of a succession of senior policy advisers.

In the short term, the 'Iran-Contragate' scandal served to
paralyse American foreign policy formulation, deflecting its
attention away from the issue of Soviet-American relations. By
the spring of 1987, however, with a new, more moderate,
chief-of-staff, Howard Baker, installed as almost a prime
ministerial head of the US administration, the Soviet leadership
resumed its 'détente initiative'. On 16 February Gorbachev
addressed a lavishly staged international 'Peace Forum' convened
at Moscow, which was attended by the recently released Dr
Andrei Sakharov as well as several hundred international
celebrities, including the Western actors, writers and performers
Gregory Peck, Graham Greene, Norman Mailer and Yoko Ono.
At the conference, Gorbachev spoke, in both rhetorical and
serious fashion, of the revolution that had taken place in Soviet
strategic thinking in recent years, with the widening recognition
that a nuclear war would be 'unwinnable', and of the need for the
nuclear powers to 'step out from the nuclear shadow and enter a
nuclear free world'. A fortnight later, on 28 February, the Soviet
leader unveiled a decisive new proposal for the elimination of all
Russian and American INF weapons in Europe which was
decoupled from any separate negotiations on the SDI.[1]

---

[1] This offer was preceded on 26 February by the Soviet Union's first
underground nuclear test for 19 months: an indication of the country's resolve if
arms negotiations failed. The 28 February offer envisaged, like that of June 1986,
leaving the USSR 100 INFs in Asia, with the US retaining 100 in America.

This key Soviet concession drew a favourable response from the new, more 'dovish', Reagan-Baker administration. The US President, seeking to regain public esteem with success in the diplomatic sphere and despite disquiet among a number of his European allies, made clear his willingness to rapidly negotiate an INF dismantlement treaty. Such an agreement, if followed by a reduction in strategic missile forces and curbs on SDI development, would represent a considerable achievement for Mikhail Gorbachev and would, by freeing resources for civilian industrial investment, significantly improve the prospects of success for his ambitious programme of economic modernisation. Already, the growth in Soviet military spending has shown signs of declining in recent years, falling from a level of 2% per annum in real terms between 1976-81 to one of zero growth between 1982-84, although defence spending continues to take up an abnormally large slice of the Soviet Research and Development budget. If Gorbachev's détente initiative fails, however, the party leader's political position will be seriously weakened and the perestroika programme jeopardised. A major resource transfer would be required away from the civilian economy towards the defence sector, with investment being made to shift the country's predominantly land-based nuclear missiles into new, invulnerable, submarine bases and to develop a costly new generation of anti-satellite weapons.

Soviet Policy in Europe, Asia and the Middle East

Mikhail Gorbachev's attempt to improve Soviet-American relations formed, however, only a portion of what emerged as a radically new, globally orientated, Soviet foreign policy which sought to de-emphasise the overarching importance of the Moscow-Washington axis.

In Western Europe, Gorbachev launched a vigorous, secondary 'détente initiative' targeted towards selected liberal-socialist countries and political parties, including France, Italy, Spain, Holland, the Labour party in Britain and the SPD in West Germany. This initiative included a series of high level reciprocal visits and the despatch of a clutch of skilled and personable ambassadors to key capitals, for example London (Leonid Zamyatin, 64: ex-head of the Central Committee's

Information Department) and Bonn (Yuli Kvitsinsky, 50: a former Geneva negotiator). Its aim was to improve commercial links and to gain European sympathy for the Soviet stand on SDI and INF negotiations. In the short term, this European offensive has proved to have had few substantive returns: the Dutch parliament, for example, voted to accept the deployment of US Cruise missiles in November 1985, Spanish electors voted to remain in NATO in a March 1986 referendum, while the SPD was comprehensively defeated by the conservative CDU-CSU-FDP alliance in the West German national Bundestag elections of January 1987. The longer-term results of the offensive may, however, prove to be more substantial if socialist governments assume power in Britain and Holland in 1988-89.

In Eastern Europe, Mikhail Gorbachev has displayed a desire to effect closer economic and political integration with Moscow and reverse the centrifugal tendencies which became apparent during the Chernenko years. In particular, he is anxious to see Czechoslovakia, Bulgaria, Hungary and East Germany supplying increasing quantities of the high-tech computers, software and machine tools which are required for the Soviet Union's ambitious 1986-2000 modernisation programme. To achieve this, he has encouraged Gorbachevian shake-ups of Brezhnevite leadership cadres, particularly in the corrupt and lethargic states of Bulgaria and Czechoslovakia. Gorbachev has, in addition, forced tighter foreign policy co-ordination within the Warsaw Pact, persuading Erich Honecker and Todor Zhikov to cancel planned trips to Bonn in 1985. He has maintained a high public profile in the East European region, attending the 1986 party congresses in East Germany, Hungary and Poland; has developed close relations with the austere but reformist Andropovian figures of Honecker (East Germany), Kadar (Hungary) and Jaruzelski (Poland); and has enjoyed strong Warsaw Pact support for his East-West détente initiatives.

In Asia and the Middle East, the Gorbachev administration has displayed a strong desire to improve Soviet relations with the key regional powers.

One key stumbling block in this area has been the Soviet presence in Afghanistan. An effort has therefore been made to foster a staggered withdrawal of Soviet forces on the condition that a regime sympathetic to Moscow is allowed to retain control following its departure. The first step in this process was the engineered replacement, in May 1986, of the Afghan leader

Babrak Karmal by the more conciliatory figure of Dr Najibullah Ahmadzai, a Pushtun (Pathan) who had formerly headed the KGB-trained Afghan secret police. This was followed in October 1986 by the withdrawal of 8000 of the 115 000 Soviet troops in Afghanistan and the imposition of a six-month Soviet ceasefire in January 1987. Meanwhile, in Geneva, Soviet and Pakistani negotiators continued to discuss, with United States mediation, a timetable for eventual full troop withdrawal.

These concessions over Afghanistan have helped improve relations with China, along whose borders 450 000 Soviet troops (or a fifth of the Red Army) are stationed. The Gorbachev administration is anxious to reduce troop numbers in this zone to enable resources to be transferred to more pressing fronts. From the onset of the administration, therefore, warm overtures were made to Peking. This resulted, in July 1985, in the signing of a $14 billion Sino-Soviet trade deal which called for two-way trade to double by 1990 and which envisaged greater Soviet co-operation in China's industrial modernisation. It was followed a year later, by major rapprochement speeches by Gorbachev in Khabarovsk and Vladivostok which offered the prospect of the withdrawal of a substantial number of Soviet troops from the 'Asia front' and gave ground over demarcation of the Ussuri river border. These concessions, which were followed by the signing of a consular agreement in September 1986 and the removal of 11 000 (a sixth of the total) Soviet troops from Mongolia in 1987, were welcomed by the Chinese leader Deng Xiaoping and opened up the prospect of a possible Sino-Soviet summit in 1988.

Elsewhere in Asia, the Gorbachev administration has made a determined effort to improve relations with the newly industrialising countries of ASEAN (Thailand, Malaysia, Philippines, Singapore, Indonesia) and with Japan, who the Soviet Union hopes will supply it with new high-tech equipment and participate in the opening up of Siberia. Largescale Soviet commercial missions have been despatched to these nations in what represents a major redirection in Soviet foreign policy, while the idea of an Asian Security Council has been floated in an effort to undercut growing American influence in the increasingly important Pacific region. In this region, the Soviet Union has also maintained its close links with India, Gorbachev visiting New Delhi in 1986. It has also begun to establish a small foothold in the South Pacific, entering into 'fishing pacts' with the small island states of Kiribati and Vanuatu.

Finally, in the Middle East, a region in which Soviet influence declined perceptibly during the later Brezhnev era, the Gorbachev administration has set about fostering improved relations with the hitherto pro-Western powers of Oman, the United Arab Emirates (UAE) and Israel. Diplomatic relations were established with both Oman and the UAE in September and November 1985 and middle-level talks commenced with Israel in August 1986, with a view to normalising relations and gaining Moscow a seat in the Middle East peace negotiation process. Relations with Iran also improved in August 1986 when a major Iran-USSR gas supply agreement was signed. These moves were an example of the growing pragmatism and eclecticism of Soviet foreign policy-making in the Gorbachev era and suggested a shift away from ideological principle and crude and costly clientship relationships towards an overriding concern with commercial interests and political stabilisation.

The Gorbachev Foreign Policy and Defence Team

The significant reorientation in Soviet foreign policy approach and presentation which has been effected since March 1985 has been made possible by a major overhaul of personnel in the diplomatic and military spheres.

In the Foreign Ministry and Central Committee departments, the old Brezhnevite policy makers with their fixed and blinkered approach to foreign affairs, Andrei Gromyko, Boris Ponomarev and Andrei Alexandrov-Argentov (67), have been retired and replaced by the more flexible, media-wise figures of Edward Shevardnadze, Anatoly Dobrynin, Vadim Medvedev and Alexander Yakovlev. Shevardnadze's appointment signified a tightening of party control in the diplomatic sphere and was followed by a major reorganisation of departmental divisions and the replacement, during his first year in office, of 35 of the Soviet Union's overseas ambassadors, including those for the key cities of Washington (Yuri Dubinin), Peking, London, Bonn and Paris. His selection also significantly strengthened the influence of Gorbachev over foreign policy making. Shevardnadze, a former history graduate from the Kutaisi Institute and a successful, innovative Union Republic party leader, was soon able to gain a firm grasp in the diplomatic sphere and had become, by the autumn of 1986, more than a mere messenger. It was, however,

Gorbachev, advised by Alexander Yakovlev and Anatoly Dobrynin, who became the clearly dominant voice. His key aides, Yakovlev (a former ambassador to Canada and head of the Institute of World Economy and International Relations who had studied as an exchange student at New York's Columbia University), Dobrynin (the Soviet ambassador in Washington between 1962 and 1986) and press spokesman Gennady Gerasimov (the former Novosti press agency officer in New York), were expert Americanists, committed supporters of détente, and were drawn from the Slavophile policy school which opposed narrow Russian nationalism. Many other figures who progressed under Gorbachev were experts on European or Asian affairs — for example Anatoly Kovalyov and Yuli Vorontsev (a former ambassador to Paris who became 1st Deputy Foreign Minister in 1985 and assumed charge of the Soviet arms negotiations in Geneva in January 1987). This reflected the growing importance of these regions for the new administration.

In the defence sector, Gorbachev inherited a military leadership which had lost much of the influence it had exerted during the Brezhnev and Andropov years. He was determined to maintain such party dominance over the armed forces and thus, within four months of assuming power, delivered a hard-hitting speech to his generals at Minsk (10 July 1985), making plain his future policy priorities and calling for greater efficiency in the use of resources. He followed this speech almost immediately by replacing a number of key military figures, including General Alexei Yepishev (77), head of the armed forces' political directorate — the key link between the Kremlin and the military — with Marshal Alexei Lizichev (57); Marshall Vladimir Tolubko (71), Commander of the Soviet Strategic Rocket Forces, with Yuri Maksimov (61); and General Mikhail Zaitsev, Supreme Commander of the Soviet Forces in East Germany, with General Pyotr Lushev.[1] Five months later, in December 1985, Admiral Sergei Gorshkov (75), the architect of the modern Soviet navy and its chief for 29 years, was retired and replaced by the submariner Admiral Vladimir Chernavin (57). These changes, made possible

[1] In August 1986 General Lushev, a firm supporter of Gorbachev's foreign policy approach, was promoted to the post of 1st Deputy Minister of Defence (General Valery Belikov, formerly military commander in the Carpathian region, replacing him as Supreme Commander of the Soviet Forces in East Germany), seemingly being groomed to succeed the ailing Defence Minister Marshal Sergei Sokolov.

by the advanced age of the existing group of military leaders, brought into leadership positions a new, younger and more technically minded generation of commanders ready to readapt Soviet military strategy to modern conditions. Similarly, in the defence industries, Gorbachev has promoted to the rank of deputy prime minister a number of young technocrat professional allies, thus strengthening his control over one of the most important and potentially rebellious 'institutional interest groups' in the Soviet polity.

Part Four

ECONOMIC AND SOCIAL DEVELOPMENTS

The Soviet Economy

Today the Soviet Union is the second largest economic power in the world with a GNP (Gross National Product) between half and two-thirds that of the United States. It is so richly endowed with mineral resources — metallic ores, coal, oil and gas — that it can be described as truly self-sufficient, with overseas trade accounting for barely 4% of GNP. Historically, however, Russia, along with much of Eastern Europe, has lagged far behind Western Europe in terms of industrial development and per capita income. The low productivity of its agriculture (for climatic reasons), the impediments to transportation and its feudal landholding and institutional structure were the three factors which retarded Russian growth during the 19th century. A number of these obstacles were removed during the last third of the 19th century as Russia's leaders attempted to 'catch up' with the West through a concerted industrialisation effort.

'Catching up' and overtaking the West has been the goal of Russia's planners throughout the present century, exemplified by Khrushchev's challenge to the United States to a race for growth which the Soviet Union was expected to win by 1980 and thereby 'bury the West'. To achieve this aim, Russian economic development has, from Tsarist times, been unusual in its degree of direct state participation. After the Communist Revolution, the entire economy came under state ownership and direction by free market forces was replaced by Central Planning. Priority was given to crash industrialisation, particularly to heavy (iron, steel, coal, engineering) and military industries (the so-called Sector A), rather than to lighter consumer industries (Sector B), and — with the bulk of the Communist Party's support being centred in' towns and factories — to the urban sector rather than to agriculture.

Under Stalin, rapid Sector A industrial development took place and the more than 20 million small family farms which existed during the 1920s were forcibly replaced by large collective farms. This occasioned a large-scale movement of people from the land to the cities. The rapid growth of Sector A industries continued during the 1950s and 1960s, as Russia's economic resources were opened out and as the movement from agriculture progressed. (In 1950 48% of the Russian population were engaged in agricultural activities, by 1971 only 26%.) Expansion in agricultural production and in the consumer industries was less dramatic. These sectors were starved of investment capital and were ineffectively organised. For this reason Soviet living standards continued to lag seriously behind those enjoyed in the West.

By the 1960s, Soviet growth rates, although considerably in excess of those registered in Western Europe and the United States, were beginning to seriously decelerate, particularly when compared to the growth performances of other 'late developing nations' in Southeast Asia (including Japan), Southern Europe and South America. However, Khrushchev wished to raise Russian living standards significantly to create a strong material basis to the Communist regime. It therefore became clear to Khrushchev that reforms were required, particularly in the agricultural sector, which was finding it increasingly difficult to feed reliably the growing urban population as its own labour force continued to dwindle. These reforms centred around increasing investment in agriculture and giving greater priority to the Sector B consumer industries. They have been a recurrent theme in Soviet politics during the last two decades. The most recent initiatives will be examined below. The success of such reforms has not, however, been conspicuous. The Soviet growth rate has continued to decline and consumer living standards remained only a third of those enjoyed in the United States in 1980. Khrushchev's economic race had clearly not been won.

In this section, developments after 1978 are examined, looking at first, the broad demographic, economic and regional movements which have influenced and are influencing Soviet politics and policy making; second, at the performance of the Soviet economy between 1978 and 1987; and, third, at changes in agricultural and industrial policies.

Recent Economic and Demographic Trends

Demographic Movements

The first clear demographic trend apparent during recent years has been the continuing movement, particularly of younger males, away from agriculture and into towns. In 1960, 42% of the Soviet workforce were employed in the agricultural sector, in 1980, only 14%. Although this figure was still well in excess of the 6% average for the industrialised Western market economies, it represented a movement of considerable economic and political significance. It provided labour for industry and brought increased numbers within the realm of the party cells. At the same time it created potential labour shortages for Soviet agriculture and housing problems in the burgeoning cities, as 15 million people left the land during the 1970s.

A second demographic development which has vexed Soviet leaders has been the serious slowdown in the rate of overall population growth. Average annual population growth declined from 1.2% per annum during the 1960s to 0.9% during the 1970s and was projected to fall below 0.7% per annum during the 1980s. This rate was more than double that recorded in Western Europe, but the Soviet Union still remains a sparsely peopled country in many regions. Population growth has slowed down in particular in the Russian republic, where 50% of couples now have only one child and where a further 33% have only two children. In contrast, birth rates are three times higher in the Islamic republics of Turkestan — the 'baby factories' of the Soviet Union — where families of six or more are the norm. Thus between 1959 and 1979 the number of Soviet Muslims rose by almost 85%, while the number of Russians increased by only 20%. This has created the threat of the swamping of the 'Great Russian' majority by an alien culture group, who by the year 2000 will number possibly 90 million (well over a quarter of the projected total population). Before this date, the number of 'Great Russians' will have fallen below the psychologically important 50% mark. It has also vexed Soviet military chiefs, since Central Asians, who will soon form more than a third of all conscripts, speak poor Russian and have difficulty in grasping modern military technology or in reaching officer rank. Politically, this development has given greater significance to the southern republics and will increase the pressure for non-Russian ethnic groups to have a greater representation in the upper tiers of Soviet government.

85

Politics in the Soviet Union

Falling demographic growth, the reduction of the population surplus provided by the agricultural sector and the southward shift of the Soviet Union's demographic axis have had considerable economic consequences for Soviet planners. With the rate of increase in the new labour force falling from over two million per annum during the mid 1970s to barely 0.7 million in 1980, there has been increased pressure to economise upon manpower use, to raise labour productivity, to introduce newer technology and to speed up automation. Since the people of Turkestan have shown an unwillingness to migrate, there has, by necessity, been a southward shift in modern industries to these republics, bringing with them non-native Russian technicians. This has, paradoxically, led to swamping and 'Russification' in a number of southern republics, particularly in Kazakhstan, which has created regionalist discontent. Thirdly, although life expectancy rates have also been declining recently, the falling birth rate will seriously increase 'dependency ratios' (the number of pensioners supported by the working population) during future decades.

Several factors have contributed towards the low and declining population growth rate in European Russia. Of particular importance has been the unbalanced male:female sex ratio in this region — there being 170 single or divorced women for every 100 unmarried men. This has been caused by much higher and earlier death rates among men (often caused by alcohol abuse) and by the migration of males for economic reasons. The other major cause has been the unwillingness of Russian women to bear more children. This can be attributed in large measure to the fact that, with 92% of Russian women engaged in work or study, they feel, after completing their additional housework and shopping chores, unable to cope with rearing more than one or two children. Cramped housing conditions and economic pressures have compounded the situation, which is reflected in the extraordinarily high abortion rate recorded in the RSFSR. Soviet policy makers in 1981 sought to increase the incentives for child rearing by raising family allowances for a family's first three children, by extending maternity leave, and by encouraging greater part-time work with more flexible working hours for women. In the short term, however, these measures have only served to further stimulate the population explosion in the Islamic south: the response in European Russia has been muted.

Regional Economic Trends

The most striking development in the Soviet economy during the last decade has been the continuing eastward and southward movement in industrial and agricultural activities as previously isolated regions have been opened up.

In 1940 industrial activities in the Soviet Union had been concentrated in European Russia in a belt running between Leningrad, Moscow, Kiev and Odessa drawing coal and iron ore from the Urals and Ukraine. Food was provided for the deficit regions of the north by the black-earth steppes in the southwest. During the Second World War many industrial facilities were evacuated from western Russia for strategic reasons and this eastward shift has continued during ensuing decades as raw material and energy supplies have begun to dry up in the west. In 1964 oil was struck in Tyumen in Western Siberia, just beyond the Ural mountains, and subsequent surveys uncovered huge mineral resources in the vast cold *taiga* of a region which comprises 57% of the territory of the Soviet Union. Siberia today possesses 80% of the country's total fuel reserves (including hydroelectricity) and 70% of its timber.

Siberia first rose to prominence during the 1970s, becoming the oil reservoir for the Soviet Union as supplies became depleted in the Caucasus region. Oil production in Western Siberia more than doubled from 148 million tonnes in 1975 to 357 million tonnes in 1983, allowing Russia and its East European clients to continue their movement from coal to oil burning while the West was reeling from the OPEC price explosions of 1973-74 and 1979-80. Production is now nearing a plateau, but Western Siberia provides over 60% of Soviet oil supplies, with more than 20 years' proven reserves remaining. Further north in Western Siberia there lies the world's largest gas field at Urengoy with reserves exceeding 10 trillion cubic metres. This field is the source of the controversial Siberian pipeline to Western Europe. Urengoy and other fields now provide more than 50% of Soviet gas production and their exports bring in large amounts of foreign hard currency. Coal is the third growing energy source being provided by Siberia. At present it is mined in the Kuznetsk region in Southern Siberia with further untapped supplies lying to the east and north.

The Soviet government placed a high priority on the development of the vast resources of Siberia in the 10th (1976-80), 11th (1981-85) and 12th (1986-90) Five Year Plans. In 1983 alone,

FIGURE 3 : SOVIET ENERGY RESOURCES

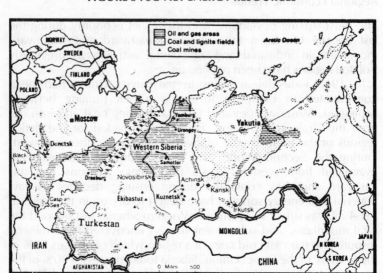

investment in the region amounted to 27 billion roubles or almost a fifth of total capital investments, whereas the proportion of the Soviet population living in Siberia was only one-tenth. The development of Siberia has, however, created a number of serious problems. The technical difficulties of working under permafrost has necessitated the utilisation of sophisticated machinery, which has often had to be imported from the West. This has had foreign policy and dependency implications. The remoteness and extreme climatic conditions of this region have required the construction of a costly infrastructure, including the 3145 kilometre, 30 billion roubles Baikal-Amur railway in the east (1974-84), the 3500 mile, $15 billion Siberian gas pipeline and special extra-high voltage power lines. This has raised extraction costs and possible sale prices, and has encouraged the development of a number of major industries at source within Siberia itself, particularly petrochemical industries at Tobolsk and Tomsk. Labour shortages have been a final difficulty. The harsh, cold climate of this region, coupled with the limited material, social and cultural amenities available in the growing cities of Siberia, have meant that labour has been difficult to recruit, turnover rates have been high and wages have had to rise to over 75% of the Soviet norm. In the case of the Baikal-Amur railway in the remote far east, many of its 100 000 construction workers had to be drawn from the Komsomol youth movement of the Communist Party.

Despite these difficulties, Siberia will continue to develop as the prime source of energy and raw materials for the Soviet Union as production levels fall and costs continue to rise in older centres. Huge oil, gas, coal and metal reserves remain to be tapped further to the north and east, while the timber and water resources of this region have barely been touched. Processing industries, including coal liquefaction, will undoubtedly develop in the future, encouraging a more permanent eastward shift in the Soviet population.

The Islamic Southeast (Turkestan) has, by contrast, been providing food and men for the Soviet Union during the last decade. In 1917 this formed the most backward, feudal region in the country, with a low standard of living eked out by pastoralists from arid *steppe* soils. It has, however, subsequently enjoyed substantial investment in irrigation facilities, particularly since Khrushchev's Kazakhstan campaign, and has become a major producer of wheat, cotton, rice and fruit. During recent years, however, water levels have begun to fall in the Caspian and Aral seas and water shortages have imperilled agricultural production. This encouraged the fashioning, between 1981-85, of a major scheme to divert water from the northward-flowing Ob and Yensey rivers of Siberia along a 1550 mile canal towards Kazakhstan and the Volga and Don valleys with the aim of doubling the area's irrigated acreage within 15 years. This plan was eventually shelved, however, in August 1986 by the Gorbachev administration, which was concerned with its extravagant cost (55 billion roubles having been spent on the project during its first five years) and its possible adverse environmental consequences. Attention turned instead to localised irrigation and water conservancy projects. Industrial investment has also increased significantly in Turkestan during the last decade as Soviet planners have sought to make use of the region's rapidly expanding population and to urbanise — and thus Russify — the native population. Particular attention has been given to expansion of the cotton textile industry and oil, coal and gas production.

The Soviet economy has been moving east and south during recent years in response to shifts in energy, food and labour supplies. Overall economic growth has, however, been less spectacular, with deceleration and stagnation the conspicuous features. The latter has been particularly marked in the nation's traditional industrial heartland of Muscovy and the Urals where a failure to invest and upgrade existing machinery has led to growing industrial obsolescence and has bred in the region's decaying urban centres the serious social problems of rising crime, vandalism and drug abuse among the young.

The Soviet Economic Performance: 1978-1987

Soviet economic growth has been gradually decelerating since the 1960s, as Table 4 makes clear. Such deceleration has been common to all Western industrialised economies but has been more surprising in the case of the Soviet Union considering the vast supplies of unutilised and under-utilised human and material resources that remain to be tapped and its still low level of per capita income. This stagnation has given rise to a lively debate among Soviet planners over the correct way forward and the urgent need for economic reform.

Two general points should be made about the figures below. Firstly, the overall growth rate for Soviet national income for the pre-1980 period was considerably above the American and West European level, while for the years between 1981–85 it was comparable to the US rate and double that recorded in the UK.[1] (It should be noted, however, that Soviet figures may need to be reduced by at least a third when comparing them with Western figures.) Secondly, annual fluctuations, excluding the notoriously unpredictable agricultural sector, have been far less marked than in the free market West. This is a direct consequence of the planned nature of the Soviet economy in which wages, prices, investment and production are all centrally controlled. The performance of the Soviet economy has nevertheless been most disappointing in recent years and has consistently failed to meet planned targets. Agriculture has, as throughout this century, been the laggard and the Achilles heel during the last decade.

The Agricultural Sector: Policy and Performance

The fortunes of the Russian harvest are of considerable significance for both Soviet consumers and policy makers. Serious harvest

[1] During the period 1960-70, national income rose by 4.3% per annum in the United States, 5.5% in France, 4.4% in West Germany, 2.9% in the UK and by 10.4% in Japan. Between 1970-82, it increased by 2.7% in the United States, 3.2% in France, 2.4% in West Germany, 1.5% in the UK and by 4.6% in Japan.

shortfalls bring the threat of popular discontent, necessitate huge costly imports (with their foreign policy implications), lead to a deterioration in the balance of payments and put a squeeze on investment funds available to the industrial sector. Unfortunately, however, the harsh climatic conditions within the Soviet Union have bred a notoriously fickle agricultural sector, with production levels fluctuating enormously from year to year.

TABLE 4 : SOVIET ECONOMIC GROWTH 1966-1985 (Per Annum)				
	1966-70	1971-75	1976-80	1981-85
National Income	7.1%	5.1%	3.8%	3.1%
Industrial Output	8.5%	7.4%	4.5%	3.7%
Agricultural Output	3.9%	2.4%	1.7%	1.1%

Table 5 outlines annual grain output during the period between 1978 and 1986. Following a series of favourable supra 200 million tonnes crops between 1976 and 1978, production slumped, shattering the 10th Five Year Plan's hopes of reaching self-sufficiency in grain by 1980. Harvests were particularly bad in 1979, 1981 and 1984, forcing the Soviet Union on to the world market to import grain to feed its livestock population. During the 1960s the Soviet Union had only rarely been a net grain importer, not emerging as a major buyer until 1972. From 1975 onwards, however, Russia became a regular grain importer with purchases exceeding 25 million tonnes in 1979, 40 million tonnes in 1981, and remaining around this level during the ensuing years, reaching 55 million tonnes in 1984 and 1985. It was fortunate, however, in being able to purchase from a glutted world market, which meant that temporary US embargos (in 1980) were easily circumvented at only limited additional cost. Grain importations, which along with other food imports accounted for more than one-fifth of the total Soviet import bill, were, however, both a strain on the nation's hard currency reserves and on its inadequate port and handling facilities. Inadequate grain harvests created food shortages in Soviet cities and precipitated a number of unofficial strikes in 1980-81, the year of the Polish crisis.

The performance of other branches of the agricultural sector has been somewhat less disappointing during the last decade, with cotton, sugar beet, vegetables, milk and meat production approximating more closely to planned targets. However, Soviet

TABLE 5 : SOVIET GRAIN PRODUCTION 1978-86

M Tonnes	1978	1979	1980	1981	1982	1983	1984	1985	1986
	230	179	189	155	180	195	170	190	210

meat and dairy produce consumption per capita still remains low by Western standards and a stated aim of Soviet planners has been to raise and improve the diet. Sizeable meat imports have thus been effected during recent years to meet the demands of the burgeoning urban workforce. The wretched state of Soviet agriculture during recent years has been highlighted by its recent agreements with India — formerly one of the major food importers in the world — to supply Russian arms and technology in exchange for Indian wheat. All this has taken place during a period when the agricultural sector has been given special treatment by Soviet planners and a major slice of new investment funds.

Agricultural Reforms: 1957-1978

Agriculture used to be the Cinderella sector for the Soviet leadership during the 1930s and 1940s. The new collective farms received inadequate funding for technology and were squeezed to provide food, manpower and capital for heavy industry development. Productivity remained low, but the absolute size of the agricultural sector and its workforce proved sufficient for it to be able to feed the towns until the 1950s. During the 1950s and 1960s, however, following rural depopulation, food production stagnated. This forced Khrushchev and his successors to pay greater attention to the needs of the rural sector, to increase investment, to seek ways of improving productivity and to introduce incentives. Khrushchev raised the prices paid by the state for farm produce and encouraged the spread of fertilisers and maize. He introduced an ambitious scheme to open up the 'virgin lands' of Kazakhstan, but this programme was destroyed by a series of poor harvests during the late 1950s and early 1960s. However, Khrushchev's successor, Leonid Brezhnev, continued with the general line he had mapped out. Brezhnev, unveiling his 'New Deal for Soviet Agriculture' in 1965, extended incentives by raising crop prices, by setting fixed five-year quotas, by improving agricultural wages (particularly on collective farms) and by easing some of the restrictions on the use of private plots. Secondly, Brezhnev increased state investment in the agricultural sector — on machinery, fertilisers and irrigation — at a rate ahead of that in industry. He continued also the policy of amalgamating collective farms into larger units and converting some into state farm 'agro-factories'.

During the period between 1968 and 1977 over 3.5 million tractors, one million combine harvesters and two million lorries were supplied to the agricultural sector and the quantity of chemical fertilisers used trebled to over 80 million tonnes per annum (a figure which exceeded the US total). By 1980 the countryside was covered with 26 000 large amalgamated collective farms (the *kolkhoz*, average area 16 000 acres tilled by 550 households) and 21 000 state farms (the *sovkhoz*, average area 50 000 acres tilled by 550 workers), each employing roughly 60 tractors and 20 combine harvesters.[1] However, despite such investment, grain output had risen only 26% above the level of the early 1960s. Soviet yields were only a third of those recorded in Western Europe, labour productivity was only a quarter of that in US agriculture and the rate of growth in farm output was steadily decelerating.

Increased capital investment has not then cured Soviet agriculture of its ills. There remain problems of soil quality, climate, production and marketing organisation and manpower skills and motivation. In particular, the pricing and payment system on collective and state farms has stultified initiative and encouraged a migration of able-bodied personnel to the cities, creating seasonal labour shortages. It has also led to a diversion of effort on to the millions of small, intensively cultivated private plots which farmers are allowed to till in their spare time. These 50 million plots (maximum size 1.25 acres), which cover in all only 3% of the total cultivated area, provide almost a third of the meat, milk, vegetables and eggs consumed in the Soviet Union and a fifth of the wool, and account for one-third of all man-hours expended in Soviet

[1] In 1940 there were 4160 state farms and 235 000 collective farms and in 1960, 5000 and 121 000 respectively. State farms are under full government control and are run like factories, all the produce being state property and workers being paid wages according to their level of skills. Collective farms operate more in a co-operative fashion, the land being state owned but the tools, seed and produce belonging to the collective. They are run by elected managing committees which allocate funds for wages and investment, but their production must conform to state planning targets and meet the minimum quotas set.

agriculture. They provide a vital source of supplementary income for farming families, raising their living standards to tolerable levels. They have, however, created a curious dualism in Soviet agriculture between the high productivity and intensive 'private sector' and the low productivity, extensive state sector. The latter sector remains poorly organised, with an ill-trained, elderly and often female workforce. Its capital investment, while having increased substantially during recent decades, remains low by American and West European standards, and the equipment it possesses is poorly utilised, with tractor breakdowns remaining a constant problem.

Agricultural Policy: 1978-1987

The agricultural sector has continued to receive high priority during the last eight years. In the 10th Five Year Plan (1976-80) 27% of new investment was earmarked for agriculture, in the 11th Plan (1981-85) the proportion had risen to 33% and Leonid Brezhnev described the food programme as the central problem of the Five Year Plan, 'both in an economic and in a political sense'. Secondly, with the decline in the Russian population growth rate, emphasis was once more placed on the movement to ever larger farming units, reducing the size of the agricultural population and 'industrialising the countryside', for example creating integrated cattle breeding units and egg factories. However, the tightening of resource constraints limited the overall increase in investment spending during the 11th Plan. This forced policy makers to seek out ways of improving agricultural productivity and efficiency.

The first approach to this problem during Brezhnev's final years was to raise the price incentives for farmworkers (particularly in 1982), but also, more radically, to woo the private sector. In 1977 the right to till a private plot was enshrined in the new Soviet Constitution (Article 13). In 1978 and 1979 Brezhnev went further and declared that farmworkers should be made to feel 'that by raising cattle and poultry on their household plots they are doing a useful thing, something of state importance'. The kolkhoz markets, at which farmers had sold produce at free market prices, were now given an official blessing and urban workers and factories were encouraged to cultivate small market gardening patches, to work in orchards at weekends and to build small dacha summer cottages in the countryside around such plots. Two years later, in January 1981, an even more radical policy decree was introduced which removed the severe limitations on the numbers of livestock that agriculturists were permitted to keep on private holdings; which ordered state farms to provide private farmers with young breeding stock, feed, machinery and repair and pasturage facilities; and which provided additional land and credit to private plot farmers. These reforms represented the most important concessions to the private sector since 1935 and their implementation was an indication of the critical condition of contemporary Soviet agriculture.

A second approach has centred around organisation. In 1977 experiments in the use of 'enlarged integrated detachments' of tractors, harvesters, repair shops and mobile canteens were begun in the Ipatovo district of the Stavropol region. Five years later, in May 1982, a more fundamental attempt to tackle the organisational and bureaucratic defects in collective and state farm agriculture was made by the CPSU Central Committee, with the launch of a new 'Food Programme' which was centred around the creation of new district and regional level agro-industrial administrations to co-ordinate the production, transport, storage and processing of food. This followed experiments carried out in the Abasha region of Georgia under the auspices of Edward Shevardnadze. These approaches were favoured by Mikhail Gorbachev, the party Secretary in charge of agriculture since 1978 and a man who, having worked during his youth on a collective farm as an assistant to a combine driver, was acutely aware of the organisational deficiencies of the prevailing system. Such reforms, however, ran up against entrenched opposition from state farm, regional and ministerial bureaucrats.

Thus in 1984, with the accession of Konstantin Chernenko to the party leadership, there was a return to a more traditionalist and extensivist approach to the agricultural problem, which recalled Khrushchev's Kazakhstan campaign of the 1950s. A new 'Long Term Programme for Land Improvement' was introduced in October 1984 with the priority being placed upon expanding both the cultivated area and, in particular, the irrigated area. Extra irrigation and drainage, it was projected, could bring into cultivation an additional 50 million acres by the end of the century, 50% more than was currently planned, and lead to a doubling of yields. At the heart of this programme was the scheme (see page 89) for the redirection of water from the northward flowing rivers of Siberia to the arid lands of the Caucasus and Central Asia.

Such an expensive, extensivist approach was, however, opposed by the Agriculture Secretary, Mikhail Gorbachev, who sought instead an 'intensification' of production on existing land through improved organisation, technology and incentives. The 'Siberian rivers scheme' was thus rapidly shelved after Gorbachev's election as CPSU General Secretary in March 1985. Instead, the new party leader's first two years in power saw the introduction of a series of significant new reform initiatives aimed at tackling the more fundamental structural problems of Soviet agriculture.

For Gorbachev, the most serious flaw in the prevailing system continued to be the attempt of central and regional bodies to dictate detailed production systems and priorities for an activity which varied to such an enormous degree by locality. He thus set about thoroughly overhauling the existing planning system in 1985-86 in a two-pronged manner. He firstly created, in November 1985, a new super-committee for agriculture — the State Agro-Industrial Committee (*Gosagroprom*) — under the control of Vsevolod Murakhovsky (60), Gorbachev's successor as Stavropol Region party leader, to bring together the six existing agricultural ministries/committees and to act as a top tier co-ordinating body. Then, secondly, at the 27th Party Congress in February-March 1986, he unveiled a radical new reform package which, drawing upon elements of Deng Xiaoping's 'responsibility system' and Lenin's 1921-27 'New Economic Policy', sought to extend the production and investment autonomy of state and collective farms. Under this new scheme, which was adopted by the CPSU Central Committee and the Council of Ministers on 28 March 1986, fixed five-year contracts were established for the supply of specified foodstuffs at set prices for state and collective farms. Once these contracts had been fulfilled, however, farms were to be allowed in the future to sell excess produce to whichever market they chose — the state, co-operatives, factories or direct to the public — and would be empowered to retain the surplus generated for the benefit of their workers or for further investment. In addition, special bonus price premiums were to be given for production in excess of 1981-85 levels. Such a scheme, which represented in a number of respects a return to a 'food tax' system, was influenced by contemporary experiments with brigade or work team (*zveno*) contracts at the local level in Stavropol during the early 1970s. The new system was, at first, introduced into a limited number of areas in 1986, being combined with zveno contracting in places, but was to be sub-sequently, if successful, extended fully across the country. The reform was aimed at boosting grain production to a level of 250-255 million tonnes by the year 1990. In the short term, however, being

coupled with the new administration's concomitant encouragement of the private plot sector, it served to give the greatest boost to
spare-time fruit and vegetable production.

The other elements of Gorbachev's agricultural programme
were more conventional. Investment during the Plan period was to
remain high, at a third of the state total, but priority switched away
from large scale projects towards local irrigation and soil
improvement schemes, to infrastructural improvement (in an
effort to reduce wastage), to extending mechanisation and
processing facilities and towards concentration on areas promising
the highest returns. In addition, Gorbachev, influenced by his wife
Raisa's sociological research, has shown a desire to improve social
amenities in rural areas in an effort to slow the pace of rural
emigration and to narrow urban-rural distinctions.

The Gorbachev programme promises much during the forthcoming decade. Unfortunately, during its first year of operation it
suffered the major setback of the Chernobyl nuclear reactor
accident which caused substantial crop damage in the Ukraine and
adjoining regions. Despite such losses, the country enjoyed its best
overall harvest since 1978, a grain harvest of more than 210 million
tonnes being recorded. The radiation leakage from Chernobyl is
likely, however, to have a continued long-term detrimental impact
upon agricultural production in the Ukraine, a region responsible
for 40% of the Soviet Union's winter wheat acreage. This will make it
difficult for the Gorbachev administration to attain its target of
2.7-3.0% per annum agricultural growth during the 12th Plan
period.

The Industrial Sector: Policy and Performance

The Soviet industrial sector expanded spectacularly between 1920
and 1975, by which date the USSR produced 20% of the world's
industrial output. However, the rate of growth slackened during
the 1960s and declined most sharply after 1975. This imperilled both
the defence capabilities of the Soviet Union as a world power and
the post-Stalin aim of significantly raising workers' living standards.
Revitalisation of the industrial sector thus became a top priority for
Soviet leaders as they analysed its causes and prescribed new
remedies.

Industrial Reforms: 1957-1978

One key factor behind the slowdown in Soviet industrial growth rates has been the steady switch in resources from Sector A (although it still received the lion's share) to the Sector B consumer industries under Khrushchev and then under Kosygin with the 1971-75 Plan. High growth rates had been easier to engineer under Central Planning in the heavy industries than in the consumer industries which required more sophisticated management techniques. By the 1960s, however, the Central Planning system was holding back all sectors of the increasingly complex Soviet economy.

The Central Planning, 'Command Economy', system as it operated during the 1950s involved a rigidly hierarchical chain of command, running from Moscow to the small town factory or state farm level, by which the broad aims of the CPSU leadership, performing its 'guiding role', were transformed into practical directives. The party's goals were formulated by the Politburo-Secretariat and ratified by the Central Committee and quinquennial Congress before being passed on to the Gosplan State Planning Commission for translation into detailed sectoral plans. These blueprints were, in turn, passed down to the industrial ministries whose task it was to establish thorough plans for each enterprise under their control, taking into account past performances. These 'enterprise plans' were subdivided in turn, with detailed targets being established for output and productivity on a yearly, quarterly and monthly basis for each workshop branch. In addition, the prices of inputs and outputs, the sources of supply, and markets for sale were strictly stipulated by the central ministries. Such a planning system, which involved the detailed regulation of factory level activities by remote ministries and concentration on target fulfilment, led to a dangerously narrow view of priorities at the factory level. The consequence of this was gross inefficiency and misallocation of resources. Production managers, solely concerned with maximising output of their own specific target, hoarded materials and labour and gave little concern to product quality. The absence of inter-communication between enterprises led to supply bottlenecks and consequent production delays. Finally, the lack of autonomy given to managers to formulate new product lines stifled initiative and innovation.

Khrushchev attempted to deal with some of these shortcomings by decentralising decision-making and fostering greater intra-industry co-ordination when he replaced the 20 separate industrial ministries with 104 regional economic councils (sovnarkhozy) in 1957. These reforms produced, however, disappointing results, with inter-regional co-ordination now emerging as a new problem. The reforms were thus repealed in 1965, when the industrial ministries were reinstated in a modified form. At the same time, however, a radical programme of economic reform was introduced by Alexei Kosygin. It was designed to give industrial managers more scope for initiative; to make factories more concerned with quality, 'profits' and markets rather than with just maximising total output; to reduce the number of planning indicators sent down from the centre; and to encourage greater intra-industry co-ordination through a policy of merger into 'production associations'. This was supported in 1969 by Kosygin's encouragement of the Shchekino chemical factory efficiency experiment, which involved a reduction in manpower numbers and the distribution of wages saved among the remaining employees. Such reforms soon, however, ran up against strong opposition from both party bureaucrats and from workers fearing redundancy. They failed to receive the firm backing of the cautious Brezhnev, whose interests lay more in foreign affairs, agriculture and defence, and were therefore either shelved or diluted as Kosygin turned to détente and the stimulation of East-West trade between 1971-75 as a means of pepping up the Soviet and Eastern Bloc economies.

The Mid 1970s Industrial Crisis

By the mid 1970s the Soviet economy faced, however, new and even greater difficulties as its growth rate declined more sharply and as shortages of investment funds, labour and energy supplies began to constrain Soviet planners.

Investment capital was being squeezed by the growing requirements of the agricultural and defence sectors as well as by the increased burdens imposed by Russia's Comecon allies during the world recession. Labour shortages were emerging and were forcing a southward and eastward relocation of industry which promised to add transport costs in the movement of goods to the Muscovy heartland. Energy, also, was becoming costlier and problems in supply were emerging. Self-sufficient Russia was affected less seriously than the West by the OPEC oil price leaps of

99

the 1970s. In fact, being an oil exporter, with oil accounting for two-thirds of its hard currency exports, these rising prices were a temporary boon. Of greater consequence was the slowdown in Russian energy production during the 1970s, following three decades of rapid growth. Russian oil production reached a plateau (of 600 million tonnes) in 1980 as new fields came on stream at the same rate as older wells, in the Caucasus and Volga-Urals regions, dried up. Coal production also levelled off, at a figure of 720 million tonnes, while production costs rose for both these minerals as deeper shafts and drills, more sophisticated extractive machinery and lengthier transportation (from Western and Eastern Siberia) were now required. Soviet planners recognised these realities in the 11th Five Year Plan (1981-85) and determined upon a major shift of energy consumption away from coal and oil towards gas and nuclear power. Soviet oil sales to its East European Comecon clients were at the same time cut back, while the prices charged were raised closer to the world market level.

The rapid expansion of Soviet gas production, with planned targets being regularly exceeded, has meant that a serious energy dearth has been averted. Gas is also beginning to replace oil as a hard currency export earner. Nuclear power will supplement gas as a major energy source towards the close of this century. Its planned extension has, however, been retarded by technical setbacks and, most recently, by the accident at Chernobyl. It is, however, energy conservation and efficiency in utilisation which has (belatedly by West European standards) become the key theme for Soviet planners in recent years. For example, in January 1985 the Gosplan chairman Nikolai Baibakov stated that 'money spent on saving 1% of fuel consumed is two or three times more effective than if spent on fuel extraction and production'. With this end in mind, petrol prices were increased in September 1981 and fuel prices for industrial enterprises were raised, in some cases by as much as 45%, in January 1982. This conservationist approach has gained particular emphasis in the contemporary 12th Five Year Plan.

Economic restraints have put efficiency improvements at the top of the agenda for Soviet policy makers. In addition, planners have been concerned that, despite the high educational standard of the nation's workforce, labour productivity in Soviet industry remains appallingly low, reaching less than half the level recorded in the United States, with laxity, indifference and idleness being prominent features of the low-wage, full-employment Soviet economy.

In searching for remedies to these problems, three approaches have been evident in recent years, a number of which recall initiatives of the 1950s and 1960s, others representing new departures.

The most conservative and traditionalist approach has been one that has favoured additional investment to mechanise and modernise Soviet industry. All recent administrations have agreed on the need to push forward with automation and to introduce high technology, including computerisation. The more radical administrations (Andropov and Gorbachev) have sought, however, to combine this with institutional innovations to ensure that new technology is used efficiently.

A second approach has sought to make existing institutions work as effectively as possible through a disciplinarian approach and through putting the right men in charge of factories and industries. As part of this approach, ineffective corrupt bureaucrats have been censured and sacked, bottlenecks in supply and distribution sorted out and workers goaded to raise productivity, for example, through Stakhanovite 'socialist emulation' competitions. All recent administrations have adopted this approach at some stage, but it was taken up most vigorously by Andropov and Gorbachev. The more conservative Brezhnev and Chernenko proved to be more willing to tolerate bureaucratic lethargy and corruption for the sake of party peace.

The third and most radical approach has sought to combine the first two approaches with a measure of institutional reform, giving greater autonomy to local factories and increasing the incentives available to workers and managers. The aim has been to give a more positive and broader boost to production and to better attune the Soviet planning system to the complexities of the modern world. Under this scheme overall priorities would still be determined centrally, utilising the new tools of mathematical, econometric forecasting, but local managers and bureaucrats would provide an additional innovatory input to the planning process. This approach was followed by the Andropov and Gorbachev administrations.

The changing popularity of and balance between these different approaches is outlined below when policy developments between 1978 and 1987 are reviewed.

Industrial Policy 1978-1985

Leonid Brezhnev bequeathed to his heirs an arthritic, centrally

101

planned economy staffed by a plethora of secure, and increasingly corrupt, state and party bureaucrats. Only during his final years did he awaken to the growing problems of the sluggish Soviet economy. At first Brezhnev looked to traditionalist panaceas, with the importation of sophisticated Western technology by means of détente and the opening up of eastern mineral resources during the early 1970s. However, a change of course was evident with the 10th Five Year Plan (1976-80). Only a modest quantitative increase in productive capacity (5% per annum) and investment was now planned for. Emphasis was instead placed upon increasing efficiency and quality. This was to be achieved, firstly, by a series of minor structural reforms which were announced in a Central Committee decree of July 1979. These reforms included a revision of wholesale prices to bring them more in line with costs; the increased use of accountancy methods in 'profit' assessment; the enhancement of bonuses for labour productivity; and the extended use of the Shchekino system and experimental brigade work contracts. It was, secondly, to be achieved by increased exhortation and a tightening of discipline. Thus, in December 1979, Brezhnev, at a Central Committee session, strongly criticised eleven Russian ministers for the state of the transport system and for irregularities in the supply of consumer goods. He failed, however, to follow this up with actual dismissals.

In the 11th Five Year Plan (1981-85) emphasis was once more placed upon raising productivity ('intensification') rather than on expanding productive capacity. Of the planned increase in national income between 1981-85, 90% was expected to come from a 17-20% improvement in efficiency. Yet aside from tying wages more closely to results, little of substance was introduced to help achieve this pious hope. Brezhnev may have been constrained from carrying out more fundamental reforms by the Polish crisis of 1980-81. It appears more likely, however, that such lethargy would have persisted in any case, conservatism being the hallmark of the Brezhnev years.

The accession of Andropov in November 1982 brought to power by contrast a more vigorous leader, who, with his KGB experience, was acutely aware of the deficiencies of the existing system and was determined to overcome its mounting problems. Andropov's first inclination was to pursue a disciplinarian approach, rooting out and removing corrupt and inefficient bureaucrats and black marketeers. A major anti-corruption drive was first launched in February 1982, by which date, with Brezhnev's health failing,

Andropov had already gained a powerful voice in the Politburo. A number of middle-ranking officials were removed in this purge. This corruption and efficiency drive gained pace after November 1982 and resulted in the removal of a quarter of the nation's industrial ministers during 1983 and the public criticism of poor managers. Factory discipline was also tightened up, with press campaigns being instigated to punish idle and drunken workers who had previously drifted from factory to factory without fear of unemployment.

Andropov also, however, quickly displayed a willingness to introduce innovative institutional reforms. While favouring ideological and political conservatism, he recognised the need for greater flexibility within the Soviet economic system. He had been instrumental in the choice of Janos Kadar as Hungary's new leader after the 1956 rebellion and showed considerable interest in the economic reforms which Kadar subsequently introduced. These included a greater stress upon prices which reflected supply and demand conditions, the introduction of incentives and wider wage differentials, the encouragement of local decision-making and the promotion of competition by breaking up large monopoly enterprises into smaller units. Similar, though more limited, reforms were introduced by Andropov during 1983 and early 1984 following his condemnation of the 'old ways' of rigid bureaucratic central planning and his call for fresh ideas to invigorate Russian industry soon after his inauguration. Of particular importance were the experiments in 'enterprise management' which were introduced in a number of industries and regions (including the heavy and transport machinery industry, the electrotechnical industry, Ukraine's food industry, Byelorussia's light industries, and Lithuania's local industries). In these schemes, which had emanated from Georgia, workers' wages and bonuses were more closely linked to productivity and managers were given greater freedom of initiative, with regard to investment, pricing and wages, within the overall framework of the Five Year Plan. A wider debate was now opened up amongst Soviet economists who called for greater decentralisation ·of decision taking, increased specialisation in production, the fostering of smaller enterprises, an improvement in management education and the faster transfer of high technology from the research institutes, universities and defence establishments to the consumer goods sector.

The reforms and discipline introduced by Andropov had a favourable impact on the Soviet economy in 1983, which recorded its best figures since 1978. Productivity in industry in particular rose — from a level of 2.1% to one of over 3.5% — and continued to do so in 1984. Andropov, however, ran into opposition from middle ranking apparatchiks who, grouping themselves around Chernenko, sought to slow down the pace of change and retain their established privileges and perks. Andropov, recognising these obstacles, directed an 'oblast campaign' (see pages 40-41) against such officials. However, from the autumn of 1983, as Andropov's health deteriorated, so the impetus for economic reform fizzled out. The Andropov administration had, nevertheless, set out a blueprint for the future, which was later to be taken up by Mikhail Gorbachev. It had also brought in a group of new lively, forward-looking ministers and economic secretaries, who were to mould Soviet industrial policy during the following years.

Andropov's successor Konstantin Chernenko came to power in February 1984 with the inclination to put a brake on the pace of change and to pursue a more traditionalist investment rather than innovation approach. His October 1984 agricultural extension programme was indicative of this preference. However, inescapable economic pressures and the momentum created by the ministerial changes in the 'enterprise experiments' introduced by Andropov forced Chernenko to persevere with many of his predecessor's initiatives, albeit in a less-than-committed manner. Thus the anti-corruption and inefficiency campaigns continued during 1984 and the 'enterprise management' experiment, which had proved to be a success, was extended to the service sector in eight more regions in February 1984 and to 13 more regions in 1985. In July 1984 a new incentive scheme commenced, affecting 6% of consumer and service industries, in which workers were paid by results to improve customer service in shops, restaurants and repair yards. The relative upturn in the Soviet Union's industrial performance which continued during 1984, however, allowed Chernenko to delay the implementation of more fundamental changes.

The Gorbachev Administration's Industrial Reforms: 1985 – 1987

The stop-gap Chernenko administration's holding operation for the Brezhnevite apparatchiks lasted barely 13 months. With the election of Mikhail Gorbachev to the party General Secretaryship in

March 1985 the drive for economic reform gained new vigour. Gorbachev placed economic reform at the very top of his list of priorities for the second half of the 1980s. His early speeches constantly repeated the need for all groups, workers, managers and bureaucrats, to change, and he was brutally frank about Soviet administrative and industrial shortcomings. The three approaches to the 'Soviet economic problem' were now combined under Gorbachev as technological modernisation, firm discipline and institutional reform became the key to economic revival.

Technological Modernisation   Mikhail Gorbachev had become acutely aware of the growing technology gap between the West and the East, particularly in the consumer goods sector which had been deprived of the best brains by the huge defence sector. He viewed the shortage of modern technology as one of the principal factors holding back productivity growth and he saw automation and computerisation as one of the keys to continuing expansion as growth in the Soviet labour force came to a halt during the 1980s. Gorbachev thus favoured the re-equipping of existing factories rather than the construction of new works, giving an 80% boost to such modernisation investment in his long-term 1986-2000 economic plan in an effort to 'intensify' and 'accelerate' production potential. In addition, he established a new State Committee for Computer Technology and Information Science in March 1986, chaired by Nikolai Gorshkov, with the task of overseeing a major school computer training programme and the envisaged production and use of 1.1 million personal computers by the year 2000. A further element in Gorbachev's modernisation strategy has been the encouragement of innovation by scientists and technicians, through the grant of special bonuses and widespread publicity for new inventions, and the fostering of greater technology transfer from the defence to the civilian sector, with the appointment of Lev Zaikov to the Secretariat (replacing Grigori Romanov) to head the defence establishment. This technology programme has been coupled, however, with a drive for efficiency and conservation so that the best use would be made of scarce resources. It has thus differed from the extensivist programmes of the Brezhnev era.

The disciplinarian approach has been the second and most prominent feature of the early Gorbachev administration. Gorbachev saw Soviet economic decline commencing during the mid 1970s when the Brezhnev administration allowed control to slip, thus encouraging 'inertness', inefficiency and corruption among leadership grades and sloth and indiscipline among the Soviet workforce. Gorbachev set out, continuing Andropov's work, to root out what he termed 'these unfavourable tendencies' from the very outset of his administration. He immediately launched a major campaign against corrupt, inefficient and ultra-conservative ministerial, party and managerial personnel. During this campaign, he openly denounced prominent ministers in public and on television for failing to meet targets, producing shoddy goods and feather-bedding their departments. The purge (see pages 54–55) proved to be sweeping, netting more than half of the central industry ministers during its first year of operation. It included the key figures of Nikolai Tarasov (Light Industry Minister), Ivan Kazanet (Iron and Steel Minister), Alexei Yashin (Building Materials Minister), Nikolai Maltsev (Oil Minister), Boris Bratchenko (Coal Minister) and Nikolai Baibakov (Gosplan chairman). The deposed officials and factory managers were replaced by new men who combined modern technical expertise with a willingness to take on responsibility and act in an innovative fashion.

The second element in this disciplinary drive was directed at raising labour productivity through, first, cajoling workers during Gorbachev's factory visits and television speeches and, secondly, through the launch of a vigorous and coercive campaign against the evil of alcoholism.

Alcoholism, which had a long historic tradition in Russia, increased significantly during the 1960s and 1970s, per capita consumption doubling, since vodka had been one of the few commodities, legally or illegally, in plentiful supply during a period of rising wage income. The economic and demographic consequences of alcohol abuse — a spiralling divorce rate, declining male life expectancy, absenteeism from work and low industrial productivity — had, however, by the mid 1980s, become so serious that its remedy became a key priority for the new Gorbachev administration. Within a month of Gorbachev ascending to power, the Politburo promulgated a series of tough, anti-drinking measures banning alcohol consumption in workplaces and at official receptions, raising the legal age for alcohol purchase from 18 to 21 and restricting liquor sales to the hours between 2pm and 7pm. During the ensuing months the anti-alcoholism campaign gained momentum, being given widespread press and television coverage, and a further series of coercive and promotional measures were introduced. The penalties for drunkenness and home brewing were increased, the volume of spirit manufactured by the state was reduced and the growth of sport, health and leisure industries was promoted (a new State Committee for Physical Culture and Sport being established in April 1986 and a COM Bureau for Social Development, chaired by Geidar Aliyev, in November 1986) to provide an attractive alternative outlet. The campaign, which was directed by the puritanical figures of Gorbachev and Yegor Ligachev (a confirmed teetotaller), sought to change attitudes and achieve rapid, symbolic results. The latter aim was successfully attained in 1985-86, when, despite circumvention in places and growth in the liquor black market, alcohol consumption declined by more than 30%. This resulted, as anticipated, in a significant fall in the level of Soviet crime and absenteeism. The anti-drink campaign, however, proved unpopular with Russian males. Its continuance would thus be a test of the resolve of the new administration.

The most interesting aspect of Gorbachev's new economic programme has, however, been his plans for institutional reform. Gorbachev made preparations for this key task, as did the Khrushchev and Andropov administrations, by opening up a broad debate on economic matters on television, among the academic community and in the letter pages of the party and state newspapers, Pravda and Izvestiya. As part of this debate and inquiry process, Gorbachev organised a study of the recent liberalising experiments in Hungary and China, as well as studies of Tsarist Russia's 1906-14 Stolypin private landholding reforms and the New Economic Policy of 1921-27. He also sanctioned the publication of a number of articles by Russian economists, for example Tatyana Zasslavskaya, advocating a freer market, semi-capitalist approach, and has drafted in Professor Abel Aganbegyan (head of the Novosibirsk Economic Institute) as his senior economic adviser.

Such activities suggested to Western observers that Gorbachev intended to radically reform the centrally planned Stalinist-Brezhnevist Soviet economic system, with the aim of injecting greater market awareness and decentralising the decision-making process in a manner similar to the Chinese, Hungarian or Yugoslav 'market socialism' model. In practice, however, Gorbachev's reform initiatives during his first two years in power, while being significant, fell short of such a radical, neo-liberal 'market socialist' approach and approximated more to the centralist-decentralist models of East Germany and Bulgaria.

Gorbachev's new approach involved what he termed a 'profound restructuring' of the Soviet organisational structure in which the pettifogging middle ministry layer of planning and control was trimmed and circumscribed and greater power was given instead both to strengthened planning bodies at the top and to individual enterprises at the bottom. In pursuit of the first goal of strengthening the upper tier of planning, 16 ministries were merged in 1985-86 to create two new machine tools and transport super-ministries, while six agricultural ministries were amalgamated into a new agro super-committee (see page 96). Such mergers were designed to eliminate overlapping and functional duplication between departments and to expedite the downward passage of instructions. In addition, it was hoped that these new, top tier super-ministries would prove more effective at co-ordinating sectoral activities and engaging in broad, long-term, strategic thinking than the preceding minor ministries with their narrow departmental interests. This new, super-ministry, macro-approach was extended to the energy sector in November 1986 with the establishment of the COM Bureau for the Fuel and Energy Complex chaired by Boris Shcherbina.

At the lowest rung of the economic system, equally significant reform has been witnessed in 1985-86, as an attempt has been made to increase the autonomy of factory managers. Gorbachev, within three months of assuming office, announced his intention to extend Yuri Andropov's decentralised 'enterprise management' scheme, which had reached 6% of Russian factories, to the rest of Soviet industry by January 1987. A year later, at the 27th CPSU Congress in February-March 1986, he deepened the scope of the scheme in two significant ways. Firstly, technical adjustments were made in the system for calculating bonus payments to give greater emphasis to product quality and maintenance of delivery dates, while harsh penalties were introduced for below-par production. Secondly, and more importantly, managerial discretion was radically extended. Factories had in recent years been given stable five-year production quotas and been granted bonuses from the state for plan overfulfilment. Under the new Gorbachev scheme the use of stable five-year quotas was continued but factories now, like state and collective farms (see page 96), became able to sell surpluses not just to the state but also, at higher profit margins, to the public and to other factories. The profits from such surplus production were to be retained for reinvestment in new machinery or spent on new amenities or bonus payments for the workforce, as factory managers saw fit. Enterprise managers under the new

Gorbachev reform were, in addition, granted greater autonomy in the use of existing funds, in wage level apportionment and in labour redeployment, and were empowered to negotiate their own investment loans with state banks. In return, they had to operate in a more efficient 'cost accounting' manner, facing the unprecedented threats of bankruptcy and closure if they consistently failed to meet targets.

These reforms were geared towards fostering a more innovative and independent-minded approach to industrial management. They applied to small firms, but were particularly geared towards larger enterprises where the Gorbachev team sought to foster the emergence of a stratum of huge, largely autonomous, industrial combines on the model of the East German and Czech *Kombinate* and 'higher production units' and the highly successful Japanese *zaibatsus*. These 'production associations', an early example of which was the large Uralmash conglomerate in Sverdlovsk which Prime Minister Ryzhkov had previously managed, would, it was hoped, purchase inputs from their own branches in an efficient, integrated fashion, be self-financing and deal directly in both the internal and external markets.

These management reforms were coupled with efforts to increase the incentives granted to workers. This was to be achieved, firstly, by extending the use of 'work brigade' contract schemes in which groups of workers were allowed to share the proceeds of increased output and saved labour numbers among themselves. Secondly, a widening of wage differentials for skilled labour (including managers) and improved productivity was envisaged to redress the extreme 'levelling tendencies' that had set in during the Brezhnev era. Thirdly, the quality and output of consumer goods items were to be augmented in future years to ensure that higher money wages were translated into improved 'real incomes'. Fourthly, welfare services were to be improved and sociological inquiries set in train into the factors motivating Soviet workers.

Such reform priorities were made clear in the Gorbachev administration's new Five Year (1986-90) and broader 15 Year (1986-2000) Economic Plans which were unveiled in November 1985 and ratified by the CPSU Congress in March 1986. These economic programmes had been drawn up by Gorbachev, Ryzhkov, Talyzin (Gosplan Chief) and Aganbegyan, following the rejection of the initial draft plans framed by Nikolai Baibakov. They were pragmatic and realistic, seeking initial national income growth of 3.5-4% per annum between 1986-90 (see Table 6). During this period,

TABLE 6 : GROWTH TARGETS FOR THE 12TH AND 1986-2000 PLANS
(PA Growth)

	1981-85 Result	1986-90 Plan	1991-2000 Plan
National Income	3.1%	3.5-4.0%	5.0-5.4%
Industrial Output	3.7%	3.9-4.4%	4.9-5.2%
(Sector A)	3.6%	3.7-4.2%	NA
(Sector B)	3.9%	4.1-4.6%	NA
Agricultural Output	1.1%	2.7-3.0%	NA
Real Income Per Capita	2.1%	2.5-2.9%	3.4-4.8%
Labour Productivity	3.0%	3.7-4.4%	NA

investment would be poured into new technologies, a 130% increase in computer production and the installation of 5000 new automated systems in manufacturing being envisaged, while consumer real incomes would rise by only 14%. This 'austerity/investment quinquennium' would, it was hoped, provide the springboard for an acceleration in the growth rate during the 1990s, enabling national output to double between 1986-2000. Such growth was to be achieved through the impact of factory automation and of the new managerial and labour reforms noted above. It would lead, it was hoped, to a 150% (6.8% pa) improvement in labour productivity between 1986-2000 and would provide the means for a 60-80% rise in consumer real incomes: major expansion of the Sector B clothing, footwear, televisions/electronic goods and automobile industries, as well as the previously neglected service sector, being envisaged.

The growth targets in these plans were sober and sensible when compared with Nikita Khrushchev's bullish 1961-80 programme, which had envisaged a quadrupling of national output in the space of two decades, that is a growth rate of 7.2% per annum. The new targets, especially in the agricultural sector, promised, however, to be difficult to attain. During Gorbachev's first year in power, labour productivity did significantly improve and, with coal, gas and electricity production booming, the industrial growth rate reached 5.5%. Unfortunately, however, agricultural output remained static, while oil production fell for the second year running as West Siberia's wells continued to dry up and drilling difficulties were encountered in the East. Two further blows were dealt to the economy in 1986, by the slump in world oil prices, which reduced Soviet export earnings by one-third at a stroke, and the Chernobyl nuclear reactor disaster in April of that year.

Faced with such problems, the ability of the Gorbachev team to reach its projected growth targets appears to be very much in doubt. Greater reform of the workings of the Soviet planning system would seem essential if the new 1986-2000 programme is to be successful. Gorbachev appeared, from his speeches during 1985-86, to recognise this and to be willing to effect a more fundamental structural reform of the Soviet economic system. During his address to the 27th CPSU Congress in February 1986, for example, he repeatedly spoke of the need to be flexible in the application of Marxist-Leninist theory and, like Lenin, to readapt and update it in the light of contemporary circumstances. He appears anxious to foster further decentralisation in economic decision-taking, seeking to create self-financing factories and transferring some of Gosplan's powers to regional level bodies, and has already encouraged an expansion of private sector family service industry activity and increased workers' participation in factory affairs under new laws promulgated in November 1986 and February 1987. Gorbachev may also seek to reform radically the Soviet pricing structure in a supply and demand, 'market socialist' direction. Already he has sanctioned higher prices for quality goods and created two-tier markets in the rural and industrial sectors through the reforms noted above. He may, following the replacement of the old Brezhnevite Nikolai Glushkov as chairman of the State Committee for Prices in August 1986 by Valentin Pavlov, soon go further and reduce the heavy burden of subsidies on non-essential goods and foodstuffs. Gorbachev appears as well to be keen to foster closer commercial relations with neighbouring West European nations as a means of accelerating the pace of technology transfer. A special COM State Foreign Economic Commission, chaired by Vladimir Kamentsev, was established for this purpose in November 1986 and a new law legitimising foreign equity participation in joint industrial ventures on Soviet soil was approved in January 1987.

Such reforms promise in time to amount to 'little short of a revolution' (Gorbachev: Khabarovsk, August 1986) in the Soviet economic system. Gorbachev will seek, however, to introduce changes in a pragmatic step-by-step manner and to ensure that firm party control is maintained and socialist ideology remains paramount. The reforms will face strong opposition, however, from a diverse coalition of forces. Old-style factory managers fear the move away from traditional and simple plan fulfilment to a new system of independent decision-taking which entails the acceptance of personal responsibility. Elements within the blue-collar workforce are perturbed with the switch towards payment by results and with plans for the retraining and elimination of 13-20% of labour in manufacturing industry between 1986-2000. The remnant of middle-ranking Brezhnevite party and state bureaucrats are concerned with the likely loss of patronage influence as a result of Gorbachev's economic decentralisation plans. Finally, and most importantly, a powerful group within the Politburo and CPSU Central Committee centred around the figure of Yegor Ligachev, while supporting partial structural reform and tighter labour discipline, fear the consequences of more radical economic decentralisation. It would lead, they forecast, to demands for greater political, cultural and democratic freedoms in a similar manner to Dubcek's 1968 Czech reforms and the 1981-86 Deng-Hu-Zhao reforms in China. Ligachev has thus repeatedly made clear his objections to a 'market socialist' solution in his speeches during 1985-86 and has called instead for a more centralised approach. His opposition will act as a powerful brake on the pace of reform in the years ahead.

Part Five

INTERNAL OPPOSITION: DISSIDENCE AND REGIONALISM

The Dissident Movement

In a one-party state, with a controlled media, judiciary, trade union movement, educational system and arts, a neutered church and a vigilant and intrusive secret police, the room to challenge the prevailing ideological orthodoxy from below in a pluralist fashion is understandably limited. Policy changes emanate from above as the teachings of Marxism-Leninism are periodically reinterpreted by the party leaders in the light of the prevailing material conditions, drawing upon the intellectual and practical advice of favoured technocrats and party bosses. The Soviet masses can only exert negative pressure, blocking certain reforms through what would be termed 'institutional rigidities' in the West. These are the realities of policy formation and power in the Soviet Union today.

However, for the Western press, anxious to uncover indications of cleavage and schism within the Soviet élite and rumblings in favour of a more pluralistic, liberal and democratic distribution of power, the activities of what has become known as the dissident movement have attracted copious attention. Such dissidents have come to be viewed as symbols of a broader, populist disquiet with the stifling, unresponsive and inefficient Soviet political system — the tip of a vast, but cowed, iceberg of discontent, which lacks free and effective channels through which its grievances can be made known. The pages below will examine how accurate an interpretation this is and how representative these dissident groups really are.

Conflicts and Dissidence: 1917-1978

Conflicts in policy choices among the Communist Party and Soviet élite were intense during the first post-revolutionary decade. Agronomists were divided over the merits of encouraging the small peasant farmer or whether to collectivise and mechanise agriculture, economists over the merits of some limited private enterprise and entrepreneurship — the New Economic Policy (1921-27) — or total state ownership and planning. On a broader front, there were the ideological divisions between Trotsky, the proponent of 'Permanent Revolution', and Stalin, who favoured territorial consolidation and a concentration on industrial development to provide the economic base for Russia's security and a springboard for later expansion. These conflicts were resolved by Stalin, who built upon the powerful and intrusive Tsarist Okhrana secret police system and employed the MVD (Ministry of Internal Affairs), earlier known as the NKVD, to imprison and expunge millions of political opponents during a series of horrific purges, which reached their height between 1936-38.

By means of such ruthless methods, dissent was driven far underground during the Stalin era, as even colleagues and apparatchiks became unsure as to their continued security. After Stalin's death in 1953, however, the MVD was reorganised by his fearful ex-colleagues. It was deprived of a number of its activities, including public works construction using prison camp labour; its director Lavrenti Beria was shot; and its responsibilities for security were now shared with the new, party-run, KGB Committee for State Security (the KGB specialising in counter-espionage and the surveillance of the Soviet élite: the MVD in non-secret police work and control of the general population). In addition, an amnesty and case review was now declared for nearly 2 million political prisoners as the huge forced labour camps were broken up and victims of the Stalinist purges were slowly rehabilitated. These measures represented a 'thaw' in the degree of state political and ideological control over the Soviet citizen. Their climax was the 1958 new Criminal Code which now made it clear within what limits a citizen could act, thus removing the arbitrary terror of the Stalin era.

These reforms still left the security organs and the courts with wide powers to punish 'anti-Soviet' activities. Freedom of speech, of press, of association and of election remained restricted. They did represent, however, an advance over the previous three decades. Liberalisation in cultural circles was particularly marked between 1956-57 and 1961-63, highlighted by the publication of Solzhenitsyn's *One Day in the Life of Ivan Denisovich* (exposing the extensive slave-labour camp system) in 1962. However, as with subsequent 'thaws', such liberalisation was only tolerated by the party leadership while it served its own interests — in this case Khrushchev's reformist campaign against the old guard. With the arrest and trial of Daniel Sinyavsky in 1965, the limits of permissiveness had been reached. Internal exile to the gulags began to revive and the KGB became increasingly active, if in a more sophisticated manner, as more conservative attitudes gained predominance under the new troika of Brezhnev, Kosygin and Podgorny. The subsequent decades have seen the spasmodic billowing of dissidence as official moods have oscillated.

Control over dissent first tightened with the suppression of the Czech reform movement and the invasion of Prague in August 1968. Then, as interest in détente grew, there was some loosening of the reins during the early 1970s, before another KGB crackdown (forcing Solzhenitsyn into overseas exile) took place in 1973. The organisational network of the dissident movement did steadily improve, however, during the 1960s, with the underground circulation of the *samizdat* (self-published uncensored books) and the Chronicle of Events (a journal containing unofficial accounts of trials, persecutions and policy initiatives). Dissidents, previously isolated, impotent, disaffected individuals, began to gather together in small groups around particular issues.

Dissidence since 1978

The Brezhnev administration's endorsement of the Helsinki accord in August 1975 created one such issue around which dissident groups could mobilise, the question of human rights and essential liberal freedoms in the Soviet Union. A multitude of small, ostentatiously legal, Helsinki Groups were formed by progressive intellectuals to monitor Russia's observance of this agreement and to publicise breaches of its guidelines. Moscow was the centre for this movement at which an eleven-strong monitoring group was first founded, which included the prominent scientists Dr Andrei Sakharov (a Nobel peace prizewinner in 1975) and Dr Yuri Orlov and the writer Andrei Ginzburg. Branches were also active in Lithuania, Georgia, Armenia and the Ukraine, with the movement attracting significant support from the scientific and literary community and from a number of prominent Jewish, Roman Catholic and Greek Orthodox church luminaries. Other small groups were set up to collect evidence on particular issues connected with the Helsinki accord, for example the 'Use of Psychiatry for Political Purposes', led by Dr Anatoly Koryagin.

Several years later, in 1982, as East-West relations deteriorated and arms control talks foundered, another issue emerged around which dissidents could gather — the question of nuclear disarmament and world peace. The Communist Party ran an official and anaemic peace group of its own which was manipulated at will by the veteran propagandist Yuri Zhukov. At the same time, however, the Soviet media gave lavish coverage to the burgeoning independent peace movements in Western Europe. This encouraged emulation in the Soviet Union by a small group of eleven dissidents led by Sergei Batvorin and Vladimir Fleishgakker, who established a small unofficial peace 'Group for Establishing Trust Between the United States and the Soviet Union'.

The Soviet Union had, however, been a reluctant signatory to 'basket three' of the Helsinki Final Act, which dealt with human rights and freedom of movement and expression. Its main interest in Helsinki had been in gaining tacit Western acceptance of the post-war division of Europe and in fostering improved economic relations. There had been a temporary thaw in surveillance and control between 1973-76, signified by a reduction in the level of jamming of foreign broadcasts and the control exerted over the movement of foreign journalists and by the authorisation of international telephone dialling. However, from 1977 the KGB (headed by Yuri Andropov) began once more to clamp down upon the dissident movement, which was attracting increased attention in the world's press through the activity of *émigré* networks. Professor Yuri Orlov was now sentenced to seven years in a labour camp for 'anti-Soviet' activities followed by five years 'internal exile' in Eastern Siberia and Ginzburg, Shcharansky, Petkus and Pondrabinek were similarly tried and convicted. By July 1978 over 20 members of the Helsinki Monitoring Group had been locked up. During 1979-80, as East-West relations deteriorated and as preparations were made to purify Moscow for the forthcoming Olympic Games, arrests of new 'Helsinki Group' dissidents — including Father Yakunin, Velikanova and Terlechas — gained pace and concerted attempts were made to suppress the underground Chronicle of Events. Professor Andrei Sakharov was placed under house arrest at the closed town of Gorky in 1980, leaving his wife Yelena Bonner as the only founder member of the monitoring groups still at liberty.

The rate of arrests continued at an abnormally high level during the following five years as a 'cold war' atmosphere developed and as the poker-faced General Vitaly Fedorchuk replaced Yuri Andropov at the head of the KGB. In 1981 the psychiatrist Dr Anatoly Koryagin was imprisoned for refusing to commit political dissenters to KGB 'hospitals'; in 1982 Ivan Kovalayov, a prominent member of the Moscow Helsinki Monitoring Group, was sentenced to five years in a labour camp; and in 1983 Sergei Batvorin, the leader of the unofficial peace group, was expelled from the country. In addition, the length of the prison camp sentences was increased and contacts with (including direct dialling) and emigration to the West was made increasingly difficult. With Yuri Andropov's accession to the post of General Secretary in 1982, there was even some reversion towards a Stalinist policy of strict control of the arts to promote 'socialist realism'. The disbandment of the Helsinki Monitoring Group — 60 of its 80 members having been tried or jailed, the majority of the rest (including Ludmilla Alexeyeva, Vladimir Bukovsky and Vladimir Maksimov) having emigrated or been deported – in September 1982 highlighted the reversal in dissident fortunes during this decade. The leaderless unofficial peace group was similarly reduced to near silence, as were nascent Eurocommunist and feminist groups. Only small underground networks were able to survive on a much reduced level. By 1985, intellectual dissent, which had briefly flourished during the early 1970s, had been crushed and almost totally gagged.

From the summer of 1985, with the new Gorbachev administration in power, there was a partial thaw in the cultural sphere (see pages 57-58) as a major new domestic policy debate was encouraged. In addition, a number of key dissidents were released from imprisonment and sent to the West, for example Anatoly Shcharansky (37) in February 1986 and Yuri Orlov (62) in October 1986, being used as bargaining chips in the drive for a 'new détente'. Such changes were, however, no more than cosmetic. The limits for dissent remained narrowly circumscribed during the early period of the Gorbachev administration and the 700 000-member KGB, directed now by Viktor Chebrikov, remained unusually active. It worked in close liaison with Gorbachev and Yegor Ligachev, providing vital support in their anti-corruption, anti-inertia and anti-alcoholism campaigns. In return, it gained an unprecedented degree of political influence at the central and republican levels of government.

From the winter of 1986, however, partly stung by Western

criticism of its treatment of the human rights activist Anatoly Marchenko (48), who died at Chistopol prison in December 1986 having spent 20 years in labour camps and Siberian exile, and partly in an effort to give greater meaning to its new glasnost and 'democratisation' programme and to win the support and co-operation of the intelligentsia for its economic modernisation programme, a major change became evident in the Gorbachev administration's attitude towards intellectual dissent. On 19 December 1986 Dr Andrei Sakharov (65), following a telephone conversation with Gorbachev, was freed from internal exile and 'hospitalisation' in Gorky and allowed back into Moscow to resume his scientific research. Sakharov was permitted to discuss openly human rights issues with Western journalists and was invited to the international 'Peace Forum' at Moscow held between 14-16 February 1987, where he spoke out against nuclear weapons and the American SDI programme. Sakharov's release was followed in January 1987 by the pardoning and release of more than 140 prominent imprisoned dissidents, including such figures as Dr Anatoly Koryagin (48) and the Jewish activist Josef Begun (54). The further release of political, though not of nationalist or religious, dissidents was promised, as was a modification of the controversial Section 70 of the Criminal Code, which makes 'anti-Soviet propaganda or agitation' a criminal offence. How sincere and lasting such a change in attitude will be remains in doubt, however, with growing differences in opinion emerging within both the administration and the KGB.

The Significance of Intellectual Dissidents

The dissident movement which sprang up during the 1970s was limited in numbers, running only into hundreds, at best several thousand, in a nation of 280 million. The movement has been dominated by highly educated literati and particularly by mathematicians and scientists, a group which has received special privileges and advantages as the backward Soviet Union has sought to foster a dynamic industrial base. They enjoy opportunities for travel abroad and have been subject to less intensive political pressure than many other Soviet élite groups. This intelligentsia represents a legacy from the Tsarist era, conversant with Western political notions and opposed to the strait-jacket of a Soviet political culture which is seen as antipathetic to radical innovation. It has been the intellectual prominence of these dissidents which has enabled them to attract considerable attention in the Western media and it has been the difficulties encountered in propagating their ideas in any organised fashion in Russia which has persuaded dissident members to direct their actions towards this wider Western audience, seeking, for example by the hunger strikes of Andrei Sakharov in 1981 and 1984, to use outside pressure to achieve their often limited aims.

At present there appears, however, to be little evidence of any widespread support for the liberal, rationalist and pluralist principles which are being fought for by this intellectual élite or of serious popular opposition to the Soviet system. Many of the intellectual dissidents' principles, like the liberal rationalism of Sakharov and the 'true Marxist' alternative of the Medvedevs, are too abstract and esoteric for the Soviet masses. For this broader group, the yoke of the Tsarist autocracy has been merely replaced by the 'proletarian dictatorship' of the Communist party, which, through its control of education and the media, seeks to inculcate fidelity and to eradicate any opposing interpretation. They have been brought up under this system, propagandised, and thus know no other. Furthermore, as is noted below, more traditionalist and xenophobic nationalist appeals have been drawn upon to give a broader base to the regime.

One cynical *émigré* dissident, Alexander Zinoviev, has gone further and suggested that, despite the restrictions on freedom and the inefficiencies of the Gosplan system, the Soviet citizen has come to accept the material security of the present regime, which is 'eminently suitable for the Soviet people'.

> 'So far as the average citizen is concerned he has his bread and his vodka, he need not pay doctors' bills, he is told that housing is virtually free (which it isn't), work is guaranteed, he is not expected to work too hard, and he has learned to live without freedom. If elections were held tomorrow, he'd no doubt vote to keep the present regime in power.'

The concluding statement by Zinoviev is undoubtedly too sanguine. However, it remains true that popular disaffection with the Soviet system is far less widespread than is sometimes suggested and that the intellectual dissidents cannot be viewed as full representatives of the 'silent majority'. It is rather in the regionalist and religious dissident movements that broader-based discontent can be observed.

119

Regional and Religious Dissidence

The Soviet Union is a huge nation, or empire, with a population in excess of 280 million (1986), which embraces a tremendous ethnic diversity. There are more than 100 large and small ethnic groups with their own distinct cultural heritages and languages and 48 officially recognised religious groups. Of these ethnic groups 22 possess more than one million members. These include the 'Great Russians' (140.8 million), Ukrainians (39.9 million), Uzbeks (15.1 million), Kazakhs (9.1 million), Byelorussians (8.6 million), Tartars (6.5 million), Azerbaijanis (6.4 million), Georgians (4.7 million), Tadzhiks (3.8 million), Moldavians (3.5 million), Lithuanians (3.2 million), Armenians (3.1 million), Kirgizians (2.8 million), Latvians (1.8 million), Poles (1.2 million) and Estonians (1.1 million). Almost all of these have been granted their own Union Republics or Autonomous Republics. There are seven important religious communities: the Russian Orthodox Church (with over 30 million members and 7500 churches concentrated in the Russian Federation, Byelorussia and the Ukraine), Islam (with 45 million members to be found in Southern Russia, Central Asia and Turkestan), Roman Catholicism (with four million members concentrated in Lithuania, the Ukraine and among the Soviet Poles), Lutherans (with two million members to be found among the Latvians and Estonians in the west and the Germans on the Volga), Judaism (with two million scattered members), the Baptists (with over 0.5 million members) and the underground Eastern-Rite Catholic Church (to be found in the Western Ukraine).

In the early days of the USSR, Lenin, in reaction to the 'Russification' associated with the previous Tsarist government, showed a readiness to recognise distinct ethnic and language groups and to establish theoretically powerful Union Republics and smaller autonomous units in a federal structure. The 15 Union Republics were granted powers to raise their own armies, conduct their own foreign policies and ultimately to secede from the Union. In practice, however, (see Appendix A) following the precepts of 'democratic centralism', Union ministries have not been able to exercise these hypothetical powers. Instead, they have operated as CPSU dominated administrative organs carrying out centrally dictated policies and plans. Briefly, under Khrushchev, more substantial economic powers were devolved to the Union ministries after 1957, but these reforms were repealed in 1964. Union ministries have since remained as rubber stamps, but with the concession that business is carried out in ethnic languages.

Religious convictions have been shown less consideration by the post-1917 Soviet state. For Marx, religion was the unscientific 'opiate of the masses' utilised by traditionalist leaders in a counter-revolutionary fashion. After 1917, Marxism-Leninism became the official ideology in an atheistic state. Thousands of churches, monasteries and mosques were closed and clergymen imprisoned and executed during the immediate post-revolutionary years. Further bouts of religious persecution took place between 1928-32, during the mid 1930s and between 1959-64. Thus, while the Russian Orthodox church with 100 million members had 57 000 priests and 94 000 monks and nuns in 54 174 churches and 1025 monasteries and nunneries in 1917, by 1980 there were only 10 000 priests and 7500 churches left. Similarly, there were 24 000 Muslim mosques in the Soviet Union in 1917 compared with only 300 official centres today; and there were eleven million Catholics in 1917 compared with barely four million today.

The official Soviet attitude to religion, as recorded in the 1977 Constitution (Article 52), has been to tolerate private worship at home or in a recognised and registered church which is controlled by the state's 'Council for the Affairs of Religious Cults'. The church thus operates within carefully defined and monitored limits, some, for example the Russian Orthodox Church and most recently Islam, receiving better treatment than others. There is, however, no religious instruction in schools. On the contrary, there is constant, state-supported, atheist propaganda. For this reason church congregations have been steadily declining and aging. The church still remains, however, a possible counter-culture and centre — often underground — around which dissidence can gather.

Recent Regionalist and Religious Movements

In examining protest movements in which religious and regional dissidence are to be found intertwined, four border areas of particular importance stand out — the Baltic lands (Lithuania, Estonia and Latvia), the Ukraine, Georgia, and the south-eastern republics of Central Asia and Turkestan.

The Baltic Lands   These areas, with a population of over seven million, are culturally distinct from 'Greater Russia' and closer to Western Europe, Roman Catholicism and Lutheranism being the traditional religions in Lithuania and in Estonia and Latvia respectively. They had been variously under German, Swedish, Polish or independent (in the case of Lithuania) control prior to their brief capture by the Russians during the Napoleonic wars. They subsequently regained their independence between 1918 and 1940, before being controversially annexed by the Soviet Union during the Second World War, an act which has still not fully been accepted by the Western powers. Today, as a result of their geographical location, these areas are well able to pick up radio and television broadcasts beamed in from Scandinavia and thus remain open to strong Western influence.

The election of Cardinal Wojtyla of Cracow as Pope John Paul II in 1978 and the growth of the Solidarity free trade union movement in neighbouring Poland added vigour to the nationalist dissident movement in the Baltic republics, especially in Catholic Lithuania. As in other recalcitrant regions, branches of the Helsinki Monitoring Group were established here, being led by Catholic activists centred in Vilnius (the capital of Lithuania) and producing a weekly underground newspaper. Demonstrations also took place in adjoining Estonia and Latvia in 1981 in protest against the mounting food shortages which afflicted this traditionally prosperous area and against the swamping and 'Russification' brought by the influx of Russian-speaking Armenians, Georgians, Uzbeks and 'Great Russians' to the industries around Riga. ('Great Russians' now form 30% of Latvia and Estonia's population.) External pressure has also been maintained by *émigré* groups — for example by the Supreme Committee for the Liberation of Lithuania, the World Federation of Free Latvians and the Estonian World Council — established in the United States.

The Ukraine   Ethnically and linguistically the people from the large south-western state of the Ukraine (population 50 million) are closely related to the 'Greater Russians', sharing the slavonic tongue and a cultural heritage which includes Orthodox Christianity. However, besides being such a large Union Republic, with tremendous agricultural and industrial wealth, the Ukraine boasts a proud regional nationalist spirit. It was the ruling centre for Russia during the eleventh century and remained independent from Muscovite Russia until the middle of the seventeenth century. In 1917, the Ukrainians had tried to regain their independence after the fall of the Tsarist regime. In recent years the major centre of discontent has been in the Western Ukraine, much of which was incorporated in Czechoslovakia and Poland between 1918 and 1940 before subsequently being annexed by Russia. Here, in addition to the formation of Helsinki Monitoring Groups (led by Yaroslav Lesiv) and sporadic unofficial trade unions, dissident activities have centred around the proscribed Uniate (Eastern-Rite) Catholic church and the fundamentalist Pentecostalist Baptist sect.

Georgia and the Caucasus   The Caucasus zone of south-eastern Russia comprises the three small Union Republics of Armenia, Azerbaijan and Georgia each with a population between 3-7 million, each with its own culture and religion (the Gregorian church, Islam and Eastern Orthodox Christianity respectively) and each with a tradition of constantly struggling for national independence against the encircling powers of Iran, Turkey and Russia. Such independence was temporarily achieved after the 1917 Russian Revolution. More recently, Armenian terrorism has been virulent within Turkey since 1973 (spreading to the Moscow metro in 1977) and Georgian dissidence has been evident with the 'anti-Russification' demonstration in Tbilisi in March 1981, the hijack of a Soviet aircraft in November 1983 on the 200th anniversary of Georgia's union with Russia, and with the activities of Helsinki Group dissidents and the Phantom group of Christian and Jewish musicians. Under Edward Shevardnadze, party boss in Georgia 1972-85, a close watch was maintained over these activities, with dissidents being mercilessly hounded and punished.

Central Asia and Turkestan   Russia's south-western republics contain the fifth largest Muslim community in the world and one which has been rapidly multiplying in size in an area which has received significant recent economic investment. It is an area which borders upon Afghanistan and Iran, the centre for Ayatollah Khomeini's Shi'ite fundamentalism. The vast majority of Soviet Muslims are, however, Sunni, and they have enjoyed considerable economic and social progress (particularly with regard to housing, education, irrigation, transport, medicine and women's rights) since their feudatory structures were overthrown by first the Tsars (during the later 19th century) and then by the CPSU.

During recent decades, Islam has been tolerated officially, if unenthusiastically, under a system of registered clerics, mosques and theological training schools. In such circumstances, popular support for the religion has endured to a remarkable degree: 80% of Central Asia's Muslims still declare themselves 'believers' in Islam, whereas only 20% of Russians adhere to the Orthodox Church. The people of the south-east have not intermixed or intermarried with immigrant 'Great Russians' and they are only slowly adopting Russian culture and becoming 'Sovietised'. The educated élite of this region have also failed to become fully subservient to Moscow in their political dealings. Instead, the Muslims of Central Asia have remained cohesive and distinct, causing concern for Soviet leaders. Fundamentalist teachings have been spread by underground Sufi Brotherhoods, while Muslim Nationalists have carried out terrorist acts, assassinating, for example, Sultan Ibraimov, the Prime Minister of the Kirgizia Republic, in December 1980. It was Moscow's concern with the further spread of fundamentalist dissent in a crucial economic and frontier region which contributed to the invasion of Afghanistan in 1979. More recently, the violent Alma-Ata riots in Kazakhstan on 17-18 December 1986, which involved 3000 students and resulted in at least two deaths, were evidence of narrower ethnic chauvinism in a republic where heavy Russian in-migration has led to Kazakhs forming today only a 36% minority in their home republic.

Soviet Reactions

The Soviet reactions to religious and regional dissidence have paralleled those to the intellectual dissidence noted above. There was first a softening in attitude during the years between 1970 and 1979, before a new anti-nationalist and anti-church drive was launched, as East-West relations deteriorated. One index of this 'tolerance barometer' has been the number of Jews allowed to emigrate from the Soviet Union each year. During the 1970s a quarter of a million Jews left Russia, the annual figure peaking at 51 000 in 1979. This followed the 1974 Jackson-Vanik Amendment which tied US trade concessions to the Soviet government's record on permitting free emigration. By 1982, however, as the gains from détente were diminishing in a new 'cold war' atmosphere, the numbers had fallen to 2699. In 1983 they totalled only 1315, in 1984, 896 and by 1985, 1140, with many prominent Jewish activists being imprisoned as 'refuseniks'. Only since the new glasnost and liberalisation policy was launched by Gorbachev in the spring of 1987 has there been a marked increase in Jewish emigration. 500 exit visas were issued, for example, during January 1987, with new, simplified visa rules also being introduced.

Baptists, Uniates, Pentecostalists, Lithuanian Catholics and fundamentalist Russian Orthodox and Muslim leaders have also been subject to increased harassment and arrest during the years since 1979. In August 1980, Father Gleb Yakunin, who had founded in 1976 the Christian Committee for the Defence of Believers' Rights, the religious counterpart of the Helsinki Monitoring Group, was sentenced to five years in a prison camp and five years' internal exile. This was promptly followed by sentences of similar terms for the prominent Russian Orthodox laymen dissidents Tatyana Velikanova and Alexander Ogorodnikov (September 1980), the Pentecostal church leader Nikolai Goretoi (November 1980) and five Pentecostalists in the Ukraine (July 1981) for the all-embracing crime 'anti-Soviet agitation and propaganda'. Four years later, in August 1985, the leader of the recently formed 'Action Group for the Defence of the Rights of Believers in the Uniate Catholic Church', Iosyf Terelya, was sentenced to seven years' 'corrective labour' and five years' internal exile for the same offence. Ogorodnikov (36) was later released from prison in January 1987, as part of the broader pardoning of prominent dissidents. Gorbachev has made it clear, however, that the Soviet government will continue in future years to take a firm stance against any religious and regionalist dissent which threatens the unity of the communist state.

A New Soviet Nationalism

While the door has been slammed firmer on organised and unorganised religions and on regional minorities, there has been evidence of a renewal of 'Great Russian' nationalism during recent years. One factor behind this has been defensive. With the declining demographic and economic vigour of the Muscovy heartland the Soviet economy has tilted eastwards and southwards, so the 'Great Russians' have been forced to console themselves with their cultural and political hegemony over the huge Soviet empire and to migrate to and 'Russify' outlying areas. Pride has been given to the 'Great Russians' through their dominance of the key organs of political power in the Soviet Union — the Politburo, Secretariat, Central Committee and Council of Ministers. The Soviet media has also been able to draw upon nationalist emotion as East-West tensions have heightened, picturing Russia as a peace-loving power surrounded by dangerous and vengeful enemies. Such an approach has been used, although not with total success, in the continuing Afghan war, a struggle depicted as one against backward and feudal anti-communist groups cynically supported by American-backed rebels.

The 1980 Moscow Olympics, despite the US and West German

boycott, provided a popular platform for the launching of this new nationalism. It reached a new and higher pitch in April and May 1985 as the Soviet public were bombarded with a constant diet of World War II documentaries and films commemorating the colossal Russian sacrifices endured 40 years previously. Even the once disgraced figure of Josef Stalin was partially rehabilitated in these programmes. The propagation of a supra-regional 'Soviet Patriotism' to provide popular support to the Soviet regime has been a constant aim of Russia's political leaders during the last half century. Heroic accounts of the 'Great Patriotic War' have been enshrined in school textbooks and thousands of remembrance monuments have been erected. The military strength of the present-day Soviet Union, able to defend itself against all enemies, and its technological achievements in space, are contrasted with the weakness of the late Tsarist state. This 'new patriotism' has still failed to embrace many of the minority groups and border territories in the Soviet Union, but for many 'Great Russians' 'Soviet Patriotism' is an important card, which can be drawn upon by the incumbent government. The new Gorbachev administration will wish to use such support to buttress its efforts to promote economic rejuvenation. It will seek at the same time to broaden the scope of this nationalism, involving all regions of the Soviet empire, so as to ensure that unity is maintained as greater decentralisation is progressively fostered in the economic sphere.

THE SOVIET FEDERAL SYSTEM

The Soviet Union comprises the RSFSR (Russian Federative Soviet Socialist Republic) and 14 other Union Republics joined, according to Article 70 of the 1977 constitution, 'freely' and 'voluntarily', into a federation. Each Union Republic has its own constitution, legislature (Supreme Soviet) and government (Council of Ministers) and, under Article 72 of the constitution, enjoys the right of secession. The central (federal) government has sole responsibility for defence, foreign policy, foreign trade, communications and heavy industries. In other spheres, particularly in the welfare and social, Union Republic governments have, in theory, a free hand. In practice, however, as a result of the centrally planned nature of the Soviet economy, the overarching authority of the Communist Party and the governing principle of 'democratic centralism', Union Republics are required to follow Moscow-dictated planning guidelines, enjoying limited room for local initiatives. Moreover, the inclusion of the chairmen of Union Republic Council of Ministers in the federal (All-Union) COM serves to strengthen their orientation and loyalty towards the central power structure. The existence of Union Republic level governments is, however, of administrative and, particularly, cultural value, enabling policy programmes to be adjusted to local needs and government business to be carried out in local languages, in a nation with the size and ethnic diversity of the USSR. It is for similar cultural reasons that 20 Autonomous Republics (each with their own Supreme Soviet subordinate to the Union Republic Supreme Soviet), eight Autonomous Regions and ten Autonomous (National) Areas have been established.

All Union Republics, with the exception of the RSFSR (whose members are enrolled directly in the CPSU), also have their own party organisations which are dominated by local ethnic groups and are usually headed by a First Secretary drawn from the local community. Senior Republic level appointees are carefully vetted, however, by the central CPSU apparatus and, being inducted into the CPSU Central Committee, quickly develop a primary loyalty to Moscow. To ensure such continued loyalty, the second secretary in Union Republics is a 'Great Russian', who is sent from the party headquarters to keep a vigilant eye on local activities.

The tables below set out relevant recent data concerning Union Republics, Autonomous Republics and Autonomous Regions, including the size of local Supreme Soviets and the numbers of deputies elected by each category to the All-Union (Federal) Soviet of Nationalities.

UNION REPUBLICS

UNION REPUBLICS	('000 Sq Km) Area	1985 ('000) Population	Date of joining USSR	Size of Supreme Soviet	Members Elected to Soviet of Nationalities	Capital
Armenian	29.8	3317	1936[2]	338	32	Yereva
Azerbaijan	86.6	6614	1936[2]	450	32	Baku
Byelorussian	207.6	9942	1922	485	32	Minsk
Estonian	45.1	1530	1940	285	32	Tallinn
Georgian	69.7	5201	1936[2]	440	32	Tbilisi
Kazakh	2717.3	15 842	1936[1]	510	32	Alma-Ata
Kirgiz	198.5	3967	1936[1]	350	32	Frunze
Latvian	63.7	2604	1940	325	32	Riga
Lithuanian	65.2	3570	1940	350	32	Vilnius
Moldavian	33.7	4111	1940	380	32	Kishinev
Russian (RSFSR)	17 075.4	143 090	1922	975	32	Moscow
Tadzhik	143.1	4499	1929[1]	350	32	Dushanbe
Turkmen	488.1	3189	1924[1]	330	32	Ashkhabad
Ukrainian	603.7	50 840	1922	650	32	Kiev
Uzbek	447.4	17 974	1924[1]	510	32	Tashkent
Total USSR	22 402.2	276 290	1922	1500	—	Moscow

[1] Formerly Autonomous Republics within the USSR

[2] Formerly part of the Trans-Caucasian Soviet Socialist Republic which joined in the USSR in 1922.

AUTONOMOUS REPUBLICS

	('000 Sq Km) Area	1985 ('000) Population	Size of Supreme Soviet	Members Elected to Soviet of Nationalities	Capital
WITHIN RSFSR					
Bashkir	143.6	3858	280	11	Ufa
Buryat	351.3	1000	170	11	Ulan-Ude
Chechen-Ingush	19.3	1213	175	11	Grozny
Chuvash	18.3	1316	200	11	Cheboksary
Daghestan	50.3	1737	210	11	Makhachkala
Kabardino-Balkar	12.5	715	160	11	Nalchik
Kalmyk	75.9	320	130	11	Elista
Karelian	172.4	780	150	11	Petrozavodsk
Komi	415.9	1213	180	11	Syktyvkar
Mari	23.2	725	150	11	Yoshkar-Ola
Mordovian	26.2	966	175	11	Saransk
North Ossetian	8.0	612	150	11	Ordzhonikidze
Tatar	68.0	3513	250	11	Kazan
Tuva	170.5	279	130	11	Kyzyl
Udmurt	42.1	1560	200	11	Izhevsk
Yakut	3103.2	984	205	11	Yakutsk
WITHIN AZERBAIJAN					
Nakhichevan	5.5	267	110	11	Nakhichevan
WITHIN GEORGIA					
Abkhasian	8.6	526	140	11	Sukhumi
Adzhar	3.0	379	110	11	Batumi
WITHIN UZBEKISTAN					
Kara-Kalpak	165.6	1075	185	11	Nukus

Politics in the Soviet Union

AUTONOMOUS REGIONS

	('000 Sq Km) Area	1985 ('000) Population	Members Elected to Soviet of Nationalities[1]	Capital
WITHIN RSFSR				
Adygei	7.6	422	5	Maikop
Gorno-Altai	92.6	179	5	Gorno-Altaisk
Jewish	36.0	207	5	Birobidzhan
Kharachayevo-Cherkess	14.1	390	5	Cherkessk
Khakass	61.9	540	5	Abakan
WITHIN AZERBAIJAN				
Nagorno-Karabakh	4.4	174	5	Stepanakert
WITHIN GEORGIA				
South Ossetian	3.9	99	5	Tskhinavali
WITHIN TADZHIKISTAN				
Gorno-Badakhshan	63.7	146	5	Khorog

[1] In addition, the ten Autonomous (National) Areas within the RSFSR each elect one member to the 750-member All-Union (Federal) Soviet of Nationalities.

FEMALE REPRESENTATION IN
THE SOVIET POLITY

Equality of the sexes has been enshrined in Soviet law since the 1917 revolution and, in terms of voting, employment and representation at the local and national government level, the position of Soviet women (who account for 53% of the country's total population) has compared favourably with that in Western nations. Women account for half of the Soviet workforce — 90% of them being in employment or full-time education — and half of the 2.3 million deputies elected to the nation's state soviets. In the highest organ of the state system, the Supreme Soviet, the proportion of women elected was 33% in March 1984. Only the Scandinavian countries of Norway (33%), Finland (30%), Sweden (28%) and Denmark (26%) display similarly high levels of female representation in their parliaments. In Britain, the United States and France, the latest comparable figures are 3.5%, 4.5% and 5%. Within the Communist Party, however, where only 27% of total members are female, and at the highest executive levels of both the state and party systems of government, female representation in the Soviet Union remains at a surprisingly low level. In January 1987, only five women sat in the 39-member Praesidium of the Supreme Soviet and none were recorded amongst the 112 most senior ministers of the COM. Similarly, only 12 women serve in the present 307-member Central Committee, there are no female republic party first secretaries or members of the Politburo (the last and only such member having been Yekaterina Furtseva, 1956-61), and only one woman, the recently appointed Aleksandra Biryukhova, sits in the Secretariat.

APPENDIX C

THE PRAESIDIUM OF THE SUPREME SOVIET IN JANUARY 1987

Chairman Andrei Gromyko
1st Vice Chairman Pyotr Demichev
Vice Chairmen (The Presidents of the Praesidium of the Supreme Soviets of the 15 Union Republics)

Vladimir Orlov	(RSFSR)
Valentina Shevchenko	(Ukraine)
Georgi Tarazevich	(Byelorussia)
N Salimov	(Uzbekistan)
N Mukashev	(Kazakhstan)
Pavel Gilashvili	(Georgia)
Suleyman Tatliyev	(Azerbaijan)
Ringaudas Songaila	(Lithuania)
Aleksandr Mokanu	(Moldavia)
Janis Vagris	(Latvia)
Temirbek Koshoyev	(Kirgizia)
Gaibnazar Pallayev	(Tadzhikistan)
Hzant Voskanyan	(Armenia)
Balli Yazkuliyev	(Turkmenistan)
Arnold Ruutel	(Estonia)

Secretary Tenguiz Menteshashvili

Members

Professor Nikolai Basov
Rasul Gamzatov
Rimma Gavrilova
Aleksandr Gitalov
Mikhail Gorbachev
Dinmukhamed Kunayev
Viktor Mishin
Nadezhda Otke
Nina Ryzhova
Vladimir Shcherbitsky
Midkat Shakirov
Stepan Shalayev
Nikolai Slyunkov
Yuri Solovyov
Rudolf Stakheyev
Valentina Nikolayeva-Tereshkova
Gumer Umanov
Inamszhan Usmankhodzhayev
Georgy Yegorov
Boris Yeltsin
Nikolai Zlobin

COMPOSITION OF THE ALL-UNION SUPREME SOVIET BY REPUBLICS

NUMBER OF DEPUTIES ELECTED FROM EACH REPUBLIC

REPUBLIC	SOVIET OF THE UNION	SOVIET OF THE NATIONALITIES
RSFSR	405	243
Ukraine	144	32
Kazakhstan	41	32
Uzbekistan	39	43
Byelorussia	28	32
Azerbaijan	15	48
Georgia	14	59
Moldavia	11	32
Tadzhikistan	9	37
Kirgizia	9	32
Lithuania	9	32
Armenia	8	32
Turkmenistan	7	32
Latvia	7	32
Estonia	4	32
TOTAL	750	750

POST-WAR POLITICAL LEADERS OF THE SOVIET UNION

HEAD OF THE COMMUNIST PARTY[1]

	AGE ON FIRST ELECTION	TERM IN OFFICE
Josef Stalin	42	Mar 1922 — Mar 1953
Georgiy Malenkov	51	Mar 1953 — Mar 1953
Nikita Khrushchev	58	Mar 1953 — Oct 1964
Leonid Brezhnev	57	Oct 1964 — Nov 1982
Yuri Andropov	68	Nov 1982 — Feb 1984
Konstantin Chernenko	72	Feb 1984 — Mar 1985
Mikhail Gorbachev	54	Mar 1985 —

[1] General Secretary (During the 1940s and 1950s, First Secretary)

PRIME MINISTER[1]

	AGE ON FIRST ELECTION	TERM IN OFFICE
Josef Stalin	61	May 1941 — Mar 1953
Georgiy Malenkov	51	Mar 1953 — Feb 1955
Nikolai Bulganin	59	Feb 1955 — June 1958
Nikita Khrushchev	63	June 1958 — Oct 1964
Alexei Kosygin	60	Oct 1964 — Oct 1980
Nikolai Tikhonov	75	Oct 1980 — Sept 1985
Nikolai Ryzhkov	56	Sept 1985 —

[1] Chairman of the Supreme Soviet's Council of Ministers. (Termed during the 1930s and 1940s the Council of Peoples' Commissars.) Vyacheslav Molotov, 1930-41, preceded Stalin as Prime Minister.

STATE PRESIDENT[1]

	AGE ON FIRST ELECTION	TERM IN OFFICE
Nikolai Shvernik	58	Mar 1946 — Mar 1953
Klimentiy Voroshilov	71	Mar 1953 — May 1960
Leonid Brezhnev	53	May 1960 — July 1964
Anastas Mikoyan	69	July 1964 — Dec 1965
Nikolai Podgorny	62	Dec 1965 — May 1977
Leonid Brezhnev	70	May 1977 — Nov 1982
Vasily Kuznetsov[2]	80	Nov 1982 — June 1983
Yuri Andropov	69	June 1983 — Feb 1984
Vasily Kuznetsov[2]	82	Feb 1984 — April 1984
Konstantin Chernenko	72	April 1984 — Feb 1985
Vasily Kuznetsov[2]	83	Feb 1985 — July 1985
Andrei Gromyko	76	July 1985 —

[1] Chairman of the Praesidium of the Supreme Soviet. (Mikhail Kalinin preceded Shvernik as President, holding the office between 1938-46.)

[2] Kuznetsov, who was First Deputy Chairman of the Praesidium (i.e. Vice-President), served as a temporary acting President.

135

ABBREVIATIONS AND GLOSSARY OF RUSSIAN TERMS

Autonomous Area   minor, ethnic-based sub-region.

Autonomous Region   ethnic-based division within a Union Republic.

Autonomous Republic   ethnic-based division within a Union Republic which has its own Supreme Soviet.

ABM   anti-ballistic missile weapons system.

All-union   term given to pan-USSR (federal) bodies.

Apparatchik   full-time, senior party officials.

'Brezhnev doctrine'   formulated after the Soviet invasion of Czechoslovakia in August 1968, pledging to maintain and defend the continuance of socialism in any country within the 'Soviet empire' or its sphere of dominance.

'Candidate Member'   non-voting member of an executive body, who participates in debates.

Central Committee   body, composed of c 300 full and 170 'candidate' members, which is elected by the CPSU Congress to assume responsibility for party affairs between Congresses. It meets twice a year in full session, establishes specialist departments of its own and 'elects' the Politburo and Secretariat.

Chernobyl   town in N Ukraine which is the site of a large nuclear power complex. On 26 April 1986 a major accident at the No. 4 reactor resulted in the death of 31 people, the enforced evacuation of 135 000 and the release of a radioactive cloud across N Western Europe. Chernobyl was the world's worst recorded nuclear accident. In the Soviet Union, it led to considerable contamination of surrounding farmland and the loss of 4 million kW of electricity, forcing significant power cuts in the winter of 1986-7. Two of the four reactors at Chernobyl were restarted in October-November 1986.

COM   (Council of Ministers) a state ministerial body appointed by the Supreme Soviet. Chairman Nikolai Ryzhkov. Approximately 130 members.

COMECON   (or CMEA)   council for Mutual Economic Assistance established in January 1949 to improve trade relations between the Soviet Union and its East European 'satellites'. Membership comprises Bulgaria, Czechoslovakia, Hungary, Poland, Romania, the USSR, East Germany (which joined in 1950), Mongolia (1962), Cuba (1972) and Vietnam (1978).

Congress   body composed of approximately 5000 elected members and the source of supreme authority in CPSU which meets for several days every five years to approve a new Five Year Plan and elect the party's permanent leadership.

CPSU   (Kommunisticheskaya Partiya Sovetskogo Soyuza)   Communist Party of the Soviet Union. Membership 19 million.

CPSU General Secretary   head of the Communist Party who chairs meetings of the Politburo, Secretariat and Supreme Defence Council. Since March 1985, Mikhail Gorbachev.

dacha   country cottage retreat for the Soviet élite.

Democratic Centralism disciplined obedience to decisions taken by superior party agencies. The governing principle of Leninist Communism.

'Developed Socialism' phrase coined by Brezhnev in 1977 emphasising the new maturity and social harmony within the USSR and the importance of scientific management and the harnessing of technology in future Soviet development.

Five Year Plan Stalinist system for organising economic production introduced in 1928 and administered by Gosplan.

Glasnost ('public openness') movement for greater frankness in the Soviet media encouraged by Mikhail Gorbachev from 1986.

Glavlit state censorship body. It was disbanded in 1987, leaving editors themselves to decide what would be acceptable to publish without infringing Soviet law.

Gorkom City Party Committee.

Gosplan State Planning Commission. Chairman Nikolai Talyzin.

gulag forced labour camp.

IBM Intermediate (Medium-Range) Ballistic Missile, capable of reaching European, but not American, targets.

INF Intermediate Nuclear Forces.

Izvestiya ('News') daily evening newspaper which serves as the organ for the Praesidium of the Supreme Soviet. Editor Ivan Laptev. Circulation 8 million.

KGB Committee of State Security (Secret Police). Chairman Viktor Chebrikov. Membership 700 000.

kolkhoz collective farm.

Komsomol Leninist Young Communist League. The youth wing of the CPSU used to train and 'educate' those between the ages of 14 and 28 in communist ways. Membership 42 million. Leader Viktor Mironenko. The Komsomol produces a daily newspaper, Komsomolskaya Pravda, with a circulation of 17 million.

kray territory.

kulak rich peasant farmer.

NEP 1921-27 mixed economy 'New Economic Policy' introduced by Lenin.

Nomenklatura system used by CPSU party secretaries to control appointments to 600 000 key political, economic and managerial positions. It comprises two lists — the Osnovnaya list of important posts and the Uchetnaya list of one million names of vetted and suitable candidates.

Novosti Soviet press agency.

obkom regional party committee.

oblast region.

Perestroika ('Economic Restructuring') slogan used frequently by Mikhail Gorbachev to describe his economic modernisation programme.

Plenum full meeting of all members.

Politburo dominant decision-taking 'cabinet' of CPSU, composed of 10-12 full and 6-8 'candidate', non-voting, members, Chaired by CPSU General Secretary.

137

PPU (Primary Party Unit) lowest level of party organisation, comprising at least three party members, which is established in a factory, collective farm, office, shop etc.

Pravda ('Truth') the most influential daily newspaper in the Soviet Union and the organ of the CPSU Central Committee. Editor Viktor Afanasyev. Circulation 11.1 million. (Only 'Trud', the populist, 'down-market' trade union daily newspaper — circulation 18.2 million — and 'Komsomolskaya Pravda' register higher sales).

Praesidium small, powerful executive committee, the most important of which is the 39-member Praesidium of the Supreme Soviet.

Prime Minister Western term given to Chairman of the Supreme Soviet's COM. Since September 1985, Nikolai Ryzhkov.

raikom district party committee.

rayon district.

Red Star ('Krasnaya Zvezda') army newspaper. Editor IM Panov. Circulation 2.4 million.

refusenik term used for a person denied permission to emigrate.

rouble Soviet currency unit equivalent to £1 or $1.3.

RSFSR (*Rossiiskaya Sovyetskaya Federativana Sotsialisticheskaya Respublika*) Russian Federative Soviet Socialist Republic. It covers 76% of the USSR land mass and comprises 51% (140 million) of its population.

SALT Strategic Arms Limitation Talks between the US and USSR which led to arms control treaties in 1972 (SALT I) and 1979 (SALT II).

samizdat illegal, self-published, underground, dissident literature.

SDI American Strategic Defence Initiative (popularly termed in the West 'Star Wars') which seeks to create a satellite-based defensive shield against nuclear weapons.

Secretariat 12-member, specialist, policy formulation body for the CPSU. Chaired by the CPSU General Secretary.

Sector A planning term for heavy, construction and defence industries.

Sector B planning term used to refer to light, consumer industries.

SFU Soviet Filmmakers' Union. Chairman, Elem Klimov.

Soviet people's council: elected local council in State tier of government.

Sovietskaya Rossiya ('Soviet Russia') daily newspaper published by the CPSU Central Committee and RSFSR Supreme Soviet and COM which enjoys a reputation for critical reporting. Editor V.V Chikin. Circulation 4.4 million.

sovkhoz state farm.

Sovnarkhoz regional economic council established by Khrushchev in 1957, disbanded in 1965.

SPC State Publishing Committee. Chairman, Mikhail Nenashev.

SS-20 Soviet medium-range nuclear missile.

Stakhanovite socialist emulation and competition campaign used to encourage greater labour efficiency.

START Strategic Arms Reduction Talks between the US and USSR which commenced in 1982.

State President Western term given to Chairman of the Praesidium of the Supreme Soviet. Since July 1985, Andrei Gromyko.

Supreme Soviet 1500-member state parliament comprising two equal-sized and equally powerful chambers: the Soviet of the Union, which is elected in accordance with population in constituencies at the All-Union level, and the Soviet of the Nationalities, which is elected on the basis of quotas for Union Republics (32 deputies each), Autonomous Republics (11), Autonomous Regions (5) and Autonomous Areas (1), thus giving a membership bias to smaller, non-Russian areas. Both chambers jointly elect a permanent, 39-member, executive Praesidium. Supreme Soviets also operate at the Union Republic and Autonomous Republic levels.

SWU Soviet Writers' Union. Chairman, Vladimir Karpov.

taiga sub-arctic coniferous forest found in Siberia.

TASS Soviet official news agency.

Turkestan traditional name for the five, predominantly Muslim, republics of Soviet Central Asia — Kazakhstan, Kirgizia, Tadzhikistan, Turkmenistan and Uzbekistan — which came under Russian rule during the 1860s and 1870s. Population of the region — 45 million.

Union Republic constituent national division within the USSR.

USSR Union of Soviet Socialist Republics (Soviet Union) comprising RSFSR and the 14 other Union Republics.

Warsaw Pact East European defence organisation formed in response to West Germany's entry into NATO in October 1955. It comprises Bulgaria, Czechoslovakia, East Germany, Hungary, Poland, Romania and the USSR, signatories being obliged to assist any member who has come under armed attack. Romania is an equivocal member of the Pact, not allowing any training exercises to take place on its soil.

zveno work team.

RECENT BOOKS ON SOVIET POLITICS

J. Alford (Ed) *The Soviet Union:* Security Policies and Constraints (London, Gower 1985)

J. Barron *The KGB Today:* The Hidden Hand (London, Hodder & Stoughton 1983)

S. Bialer *Stalin's Successors:* Leadership Stability and Change in the Soviet Union (Cambridge, Cambridge University Press 1980)

G.W. Breslauer *Khrushchev and Brezhnev as Leaders:* Building Authority in Soviet Politics (London, Allen & Unwin 1982)

A. Brown & M. Kaser *Soviet Policy for the 1980s* (London, Macmillan 1982)

R.F. Byrnes *After Brezhnev:* Sources of Soviet Conduct in the 1980s (Bloomington, Indiana University Press 1983)

S.F. Cohen *Rethinking the Soviet Experience:* Politics and Society since 1917 (Oxford, Oxford University Press 1985)

R. Conquest *The Harvest of Sorrow* (London, Hutchinson 1986)

W.R. Corson & R.T. Crowley *The New KGB:* Engine of Soviet Power (London, Wheatsheaf/Harvester 1985)

R.V. Daniels *Russia:* The Roots of Confrontation (Cambridge, Mass., Harvard University Press 1985)

J.A. Dellenbrant *Regional Differences in the Soviet Union:* A Quantitative Inquiry into the Development of the Soviet Republics (Uppsala Research Centre for Soviet and E European Studies, Uppsala University 1977)

P. Dibb *The Soviet Union:* The Incomplete Superpower (Chicago, University of Illinois Press 1986)

J.B. Dunlop *The Faces of Contemporary Russian Nationalism* (Princeton, New Jersey, Princeton University Press 1983)

M. Ebon *The Andropov File:* The Life and Ideas of Yuri Andropov (London, Sidgwick & Jackson 1983)

T. Gustafson *Reform in Soviet Politics:* The Lessons of Recent Policies on Land and Water (Cambridge, Cambridge University Press 1981)

R.J. Hill *Soviet Union: Politics, Economics and Society:* From Lenin to Gorbachev (London, Frances Pinter 1985)

R.J. Hill & P. Frank *The Soviet Communist Party* (London, Allen & Unwin 1983)

G. Hosking *A History of the Soviet Union* (London, Fontana Original 1985)

J.F. Hough *Soviet Leadership in Transition* (Washington D.C., Brookings Institution 1980)

E.M. Jacobs (Ed) *Soviet Local Politics and Government* (London, Allen & Unwin 1983)

C. Keeble (Ed) *The Soviet State:* The Domestic Roots of Foreign Policy (London, Gower 1985)

D.D. Kelley (Ed) *Soviet Politics in the Brezhnev Era* (New York, Praeger 1980)

D. Lane *Economy and Society in the USSR* (Oxford, Basil Blackwell 1985)

D. Lane *State and Politics in the USSR* (Oxford, Basil Blackwell 1985)

M. Lewin *The Making of the Soviet System* (London, Methuen 1985)

T.Lowenhardt *Decision Making in Soviet Politics* (London, Macmillan 1981)

M. McCauley (Ed) *The Soviet Union after Brezhnev* (London, Heinemann 1983)

Z. Medvedev *Andropov* (Oxford, Basil Blackwell 1983)

Z. Medvedev *Gorbachev* (Oxford, Basil Blackwell 1986)

P.J. Murphy *Brezhnev:* Soviet Politician (Jefferson N.C., McFarland Folkestone 1981)

J.L. Nogee *Soviet Politics:* Russia after Brezhnev (London, Holt-Saunders 1985)

J.L. Nogee & R.H. Donaldson *Soviet Foreign Policy since the Second World War* (New York, Pergamon Press 1981)

A. Nove *The Soviet Economic System* (London, Allen & Unwin 1980)

R. Owen *Crisis in the Kremlin* (London, Gollancz 1986)

C. Schmidt-Hauer *Gorbachev:* The Path to Power (London, Pan Books 1986)

M.S. Shatz *Soviet Dissent in Historical Perspective* (Cambridge, Cambridge University Press 1980)

D.K. Shipler *Russia: Broken Idols, Solemn Dreams* (London, MacDonald 1984)

J. Steele *World Power: Soviet Foreign Policy under Brezhnev and Andropov* (London, Joseph 1983)

J. Steele *The Limits of Soviet Power:* The Kremlin's Foreign Policy, Brezhnev to Chernenko (London, Penguin 1985)

J. Steele & E. Abraham *Andropov in Power* (London, Martin Robertson 1984)

M. Walker *The Waking Giant:* The Soviet Union in the Gorbachev Era (London, Joseph 1986)

A. Zinoviev *Homo Sovieticus* (London, Gollancz 1985)

A. Zinoviev *The Reality of Communism* (London, Paladin 1985)

CHRONOLOGY OF RECENT EVENTS 1977-87

1977 May, New Constitution; Brezhnev becomes President.
1978 Year of Iranian Revolution. July, death of Kulakov. Nov, major Politburo reshuffle.
1979 March, Supreme Soviet elections. June, SALT II signed. Dec, invasion of Afghanistan; dissident crackdown begins in earnest.
1980 Year of Polish Crisis and US Sanctions. June, Moscow Olympics. Oct, Kosygin retires as Prime Minister, being replaced by Tikhonov.
1981 Jan, accession of Ronald Reagan as US President; Feb, 26th Party Congress, 11th Five Year Plan. Dec, martial law imposed in Poland.
1982 Jan, death of Suslov. Nov, death of Brezhnev and election of Andropov as new CPSU General Secretary. Dec, Politburo reshuffle.
1983 Corruption and oblast campaigns. June, Andropov becomes President; Politburo reshuffle. Sept, S Korean airliner shot down. Nov, deployment of Cruise and Pershing-II missiles in Western Europe and end of Geneva arms talks. Dec, Politburo reshuffle.
1984 Feb, death of Andropov and election of Chernenko as new CPSU General Secretary. April, Chernenko elected President. Sept, Gromyko-Reagan meeting. Oct, Land Improvement Programme launched. Nov, Reagan re-elected as US President. Death of Ustinov.
1985 March, death of Chernenko and election of Gorbachev as new CPSU General Secretary; reopening of Geneva arms talks. April, Warsaw Pact Renewal Meeting; corruption purges and oblast campaign launched; Politburo reshuffle. July, further reshuffle — Gromyko elected President, Shevardnadze Foreign Secretary, Romanov ousted. Sept, Tikhonov resigns as Prime Minister being replaced by Ryzkhov. Nov, Gorbachev-Reagan Geneva summit.
1986 Feb, Grishin removed from Politburo. Feb-March, 27th Party Congress — Politburo and major Secretariat and Central Committee changes, new 12th Five Year Plan, amended Party Rules and Programme and 15-Year Economic Plan. April, Chernobyl nuclear disaster. Oct, Gorbachev-Reagan mini-summit in Iceland; Dec, Kunayev ousted as Kazakh leader — Alma Ata riots; Dr Sakharov released from internal exile in Gorky.
1987 Jan, 140 dissidents pardoned; Central Committee Plenum — Kunayev removed from Politburo, Gorbachev proposes major 'democratisation reforms'. Feb, international 'Peace Forum' at Moscow; underground nuclear testing resumed by USSR after 19-month moratorium; INF 'zero option' proposal tabled by Soviet negotiators in Geneva.

Chambers Reference Series

CHAMBERS WORLD GAZETTEER

Editor Dr. David Munro

The international directory of facts,
figures, people and places. Over 800 pages
packed with information; 20,000 towns and
cities featured; profiles of every nation in
the world; 150 maps of key political and
administrative divisions; a 120 page atlas in
full colour.

Chambers Commerce Series

The Business of Government

J. Denis Derbyshire

A clear, easy-to-follow explanation of what British government is, how it works in practice and how it influences business procedures.

The Business of Government covers the essential elements of key syllabuses in politics and public administration including BTEC, GCSE, RSA, O/Standard Grade Modern Studies and SCOTVEC plus other modular courses.

- **SIMPLE, READILY UNDERSTOOD LAYOUT**

- **HELPFUL JARGON-FREE LANGUAGE**

- **FREQUENT SELF-ASSESSMENT QUESTIONS**